SAS® SQL 1: Essentials

Course Notes

SAS® SQL 1: Essentials Course Notes was developed by Davetta Dunlap, Marya Ilgen-Lieth, and Richard Bell. Additional contributions were made by Randall Cates, Brian Gayle, Marty Hobbs, Mark Jordan, Kathy Kiraly, Linda Mitterling, Lorilyn Russell, and Kathy Passarella. Editing and production support was provided by the Curriculum Development and Support Department.

SAS and all other SAS Institute Inc. product or service names are registered trademarks or trademarks of SAS Institute Inc. in the USA and other countries. ® indicates USA registration. Other brand and product names are trademarks of their respective companies.

SAS® SQL 1: Essentials Course Notes

Book code E2359, course code LWSQL1/SQL1, prepared date 18Feb2013.   LWSQL1_003

ISBN 978-1-61290-546-4

Table of Contents

Course Description

This course teaches you how to process SAS data using Structured Query Language (SQL).

To learn more...

For information on other courses in the curriculum, contact the SAS Education Division at 1-800-333-7660, or send e-mail to training@sas.com. You can also find this information on the Web at support.sas.com/training/ as well as in the Training Course Catalog.

For a list of other SAS books that relate to the topics covered in this Course Notes, USA customers can contact our SAS Publishing Department at 1-800-727-3228 or send e-mail to sasbook@sas.com. Customers outside the USA, please contact your local SAS office.

Also, see the Publications Catalog on the Web at support.sas.com/pubs for a complete list of books and a convenient order form.

Prerequisites

Before attending this class, you should be able to

- submit SAS programs on your operating system
- create and access SAS data sets
- use arithmetic, comparison, and logical operators
- invoke SAS procedures.

You can gain this experience from the SAS® Programming 1: Essentials course. No knowledge of SQL is necessary.

Chapter 1 Introduction

1.1 An Overview of SAS Foundation

Objectives

- Characterize SAS software.
- Describe the functionality of Base SAS and SAS Foundation tools.

3

What Is SAS?

SAS is a suite of business solutions and technologies to help organizations solve business problems.

4

What Can You Do with SAS?

SAS software enables you to do the following:

- access data across multiple sources
- manage data
- perform sophisticated analyses
- deliver information across your organization

5

What Is Base SAS?

Base SAS is the centerpiece of all SAS software.

Base SAS provides

- a highly flexible, highly extensible fourth-generation programming language
- a rich library of encapsulated programming procedures
- a graphic user interface for administering SAS tasks.

6

About This Class

This class focuses on the SAS implementation of the Structured Query Language, PROC SQL. This procedure provides the functionality to

- write basic reports
- create new columns
- join tables
- create data sets and views
- create macro variables
- and more.

7

1.01 Multiple Choice Poll

Have you worked with PROC SQL?

a. yes, just maintaining programs

b. yes, writing some programs

c. no, not at all

8

1.2 Course Logistics

Objectives

- Describe the data used in the course.
- Designate the editors and processing mode available for workshops.
- Specify the naming convention used for course files.
- Define the three levels of exercises.
- Navigate the Help facility.

11

Orion Star Sports & Outdoors

This course focuses on a fictitious global sports and outdoors retailer that has traditional stores, an online store, and a large catalog business.

12

Orion Star Data

Large amounts of data are stored in transactional systems in various formats.

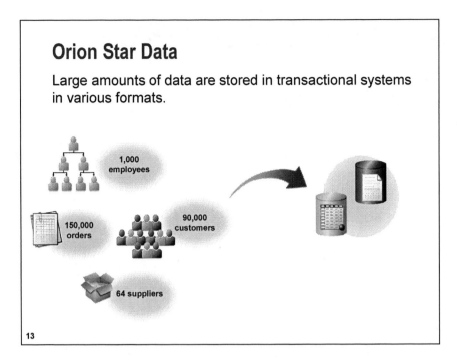

13

Orion Star Business Scenarios

In this course, you *write* SAS programs that access Orion Star data and create reports using an editor.

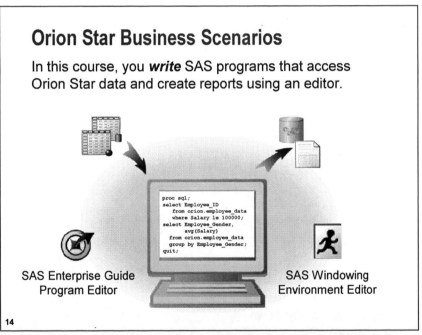

SAS Enterprise Guide
Program Editor

SAS Windowing
Environment Editor

14

	SAS Enterprise Guide	SAS Windowing Environment
Editor	Program Editor	Enhanced Editor or Program Editor
Formatting	Automatic	Manual
Syntax Help	Context-sensitive	Menu- or function key-based
Output	SAS Report	HTML

	SAS Enterprise Guide	SAS Windowing Environment
Projects	Yes	No
Autocomplete	Yes	No
Program Flow Analysis	Yes	No

What Is SAS Enterprise Guide?

 SAS Enterprise Guide is a powerful Windows client application that provides a GUI for transparently accessing the power of SAS.

It provides the following:
- a point-and-click interface with menus and wizards that enable the user to define tasks
- SAS code generation and execution based on user selections
- a full programming interface that can be used to write, edit, and submit SAS code

✎ This class uses the programming interface.

15

What Is the SAS Windowing Environment?

 The *SAS windowing environment* consists of a series of windows that you can use to edit and submit programs, and view the results.

The SAS windowing environment editor contains the following windows:
- the Enhanced Editor and Program Editor windows for preparing and submitting a program
- the Log window for viewing notes, warning messages, and error messages
- the Output window, which contains the output generated by most SAS procedures

16

1.02 Poll

Which editor will you use to write SAS programs?

a. SAS Enterprise Guide Program Editor
b. the Program Editor in the SAS windowing environment
c. a different editor
d. I do not know

17

Running SAS Programs

In this course, you invoke SAS in interactive mode (SAS Enterprise Guide or windowing environment) to *process* programs.

18

Running SAS Programs

There are other modes for processing SAS programs.

Batch Mode for z/OS (OS/390)	Noninteractive Mode

Use any editor to create a file with SAS statements plus job control statements (JCL), and then submit the file to the operating system.
 	
Example file:
 	
`//JOBNAME JOB …`
`// EXEC SAS`
`//SYSIN DD *`
 	
`proc freq data=x.pay;`
`    tables ID;`
`run;`
	Use any editor to create a file with SAS statements, and then issue the SAS command referencing the file.
	
	Directory-based example:
	
	SAS *filename*
	
	z/OS (OS/390) example:
	
	SAS INPUT(*filename*)

19

Program Naming Conventions

In this course, you retrieve and save SAS programs using the structure below.

❶ course ID
❷ chapter #
❸ type
    a=activity
    d=demo
    e=exercise
    s=solution
❹ item #
❺ placeholder

s104d01x
❶ ❷ ❸ ❹ ❺

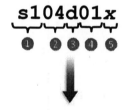

SQL1, Chapter 4, Demo 1

20

Filename and Library Name References

In this course, macro variable references are used to give a more flexible approach for locating files.
Examples:

```
%let path=s:\workshop;
libname orion "s:\workshop";
```

21

Three Levels of Exercises

The course is designed to have you complete only *one* set of exercises. Select the level most appropriate for your skill set.

Level 1	Provides step-by-step instructions.
Level 2	Provides less information and guidance.
Challenge	Provides minimal information and guidance. Students might need to use the Help facility.

22

Getting Help

In class, you can get product help in several ways, depending on the editor being used.

- Getting Started tutorials
- Help facilities included in the software
- Web-based help, if web access is available

23

Extending Your Learning

After class, you will have access to an extended learning page that was created for this course. The page includes

- course data and program files
- a PDF file of the course notes
- other course-specific resources.

✏ This page might also be available during class.

24

1.3 Course Data Files

Objectives

- Execute a SAS program to create the course data files.
- Execute a SAS program to define the data location.

26

Business Scenario

Identify a location for the course data files and execute programs to create the files and define the location.

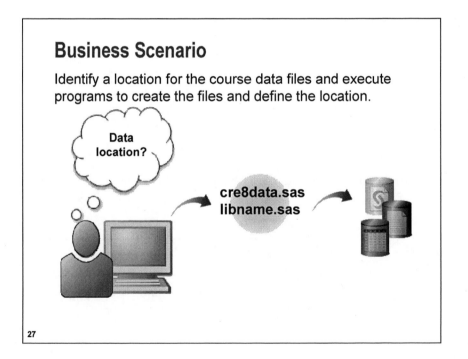

Data location?

cre8data.sas
libname.sas

27

Creating Course Data Files

cre8data

The **cre8data** program creates data files for this course. The program must be executed once, at the start of the *course*.

1. Define the target location for your course data files. The default location for all course data is **s:\workshop**. If your data files are to be created in a location other than **s:\workshop**, you must identify a location for the SAS data files.

   Create the SAS data files here: _____

2. Select **File ⇨ Open ⇨ Program**.

3. If necessary, navigate to the data folder.

4. Select **cre8data** and click **Open**. The program is displayed in an editor.

   Note the default value for the %LET statement.

   If your files are to be created at a location other than **s:\workshop**, in the %LET statement, change the value assigned to PATH= to reflect the location of the SAS data files.

   ✎ If your files are to be created in **s:\workshop**, then no change is needed.

5. Press F3 to submit the program.

6. View the log and verify that there are no errors.

7. View the results and verify that the output contains a list of data files.

Defining the Data Location

libname

The **libname** program tells SAS where to find the course data files. This program must be executed each time you start a new *session*.

1. Open the **libname** program.

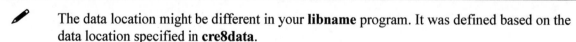

```
%let path=s:\workshop;
libname orion "s:\workshop";
```

   ✎ The data location might be different in your **libname** program. It was defined based on the data location specified in **cre8data**.

2. Press F3 to submit the **libname** program.

3. View the log and verify that there are no errors or warnings.

Exercises

 You **must** complete the exercises to create the course data files. If you do not create the data files, all programs in this course will fail.

Required Exercise

1. **Creating Course Data**

   a. The default location for all course data is **s:\workshop**. If your data files are to be created in a location other than **s:\workshop**, you must identify a location for your SAS data files.

   Create the SAS data files here: _____

   b. Select **File** ⇨ **Open** ⇨ **Program**.

   c. Navigate to the data folder, select **cre8data**, and click **Open**. The program is displayed in an editor.

   Observe the default value for the %LET statement.

```
/* Windows/UNIX */

/* STEP 1: Notice the default values for the %LET statements. */

/* STEP 2: If your files are not to be located in S:\workshop */
/* change the value of PATH= %LET statement to reflect */
/* your data location. */

/* STEP 3: Submit the program to create the course data files. */

/* STEP 4: Go to the Results-SAS Report tab in Enterprise Guide*/
/* or the Results Viewer in SAS and verify the CONTENTS procedure*/
/* report lists the names of the SAS data sets that were created.*/

%let path=s:\workshop;


/*++++++++++++++++++++++++++++++++++++++++++++++++++++++*/
/* WARNING: DO NOT ALTER CODE BELOW THIS LINE */
/*++++++++++++++++++++++++++++++++++++++++++++++++++++++*/
```

   If your files are to be created at a location other than **s:\workshop**, in the %LET statement, change the value assigned to PATH= to reflect the location of the SAS data files.

   ✎ If your files are to be created in **s:\workshop**, then no change is needed.

   d. Press F3 to submit the program.

   e. View the log and verify that there are no errors.

f. View the results and verify that the output contains a list of data files, similar to the list below:

The SAS System

The CONTENTS Procedure

Directory	
Libref	ORION
Engine	V9
Physical Name	s:\workshop
Filename	s:\workshop

#	Name	Member Type	File Size	Last Modified
1	CUSTOMER	DATA	33792	17Oct12:12:23:14
2	CUSTOMER_TYPE	DATA	17408	17Oct12:12:23:19
	CUSTOMER_TYPE	INDEX	9216	17Oct12:12:23:19
3	EMPLOYEES	DATA	25600	17Oct12:12:23:15

2. Defining the Data Location

a. Open the **libname** program. Do not change anything in this program.

b. Submit the program.

c. View the log and verify that there are no errors or warnings.

1.4 Introducing the Structured Query Language

Objectives

- Describe the historical development of Structured Query Language (SQL).
- Explain how SQL is used.

31

Structured Query Language

Structured Query Language (SQL) is a standardized language originally designed as a relational database query tool.

SQL is currently used in many software products to retrieve and update data.

```
proc sql;
select Employee_ID
    from orion.employee_data
    where Salary le 100000;
select Employee_Gender,
    avg(Salary)
    from orion.employee_data
    group by Employee_Gender;
quit;
```

32

Structured Query Language: Timeline

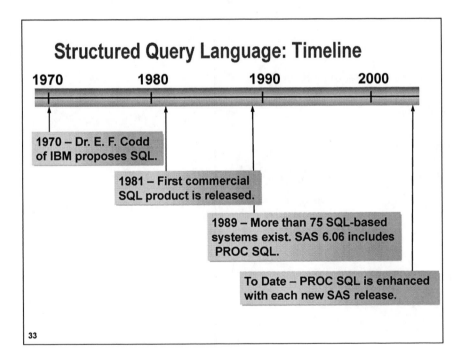

1970 – Dr. E. F. Codd of IBM proposes SQL.

1981 – First commercial SQL product is released.

1989 – More than 75 SQL-based systems exist. SAS 6.06 includes PROC SQL.

To Date – PROC SQL is enhanced with each new SAS release.

33

Relational Data

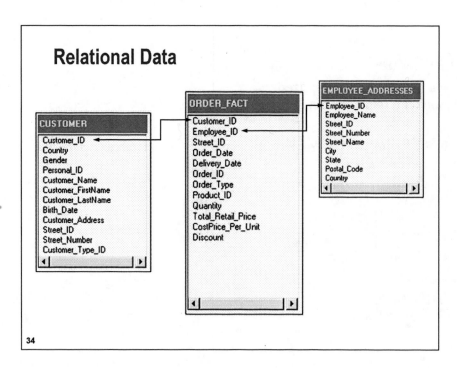

34

SQL Procedure

The SAS SQL procedure enables the use of SQL in SAS.

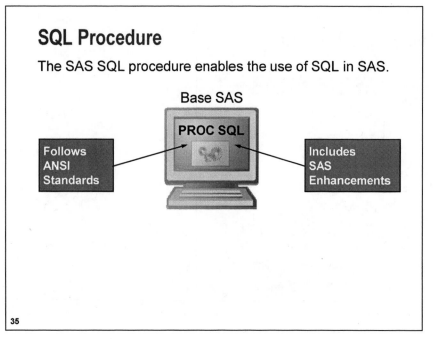

35

SQL Procedure

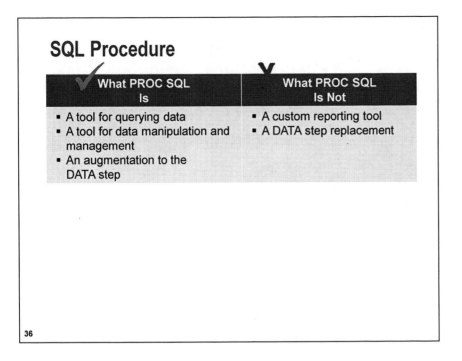

✓ What PROC SQL Is	✗ What PROC SQL Is Not
• A tool for querying data • A tool for data manipulation and management • An augmentation to the DATA step	• A custom reporting tool • A DATA step replacement

36

SQL Procedure versus Traditional SAS

The SQL procedure can sometimes reproduce the results of multiple DATA and procedure steps with a single query.

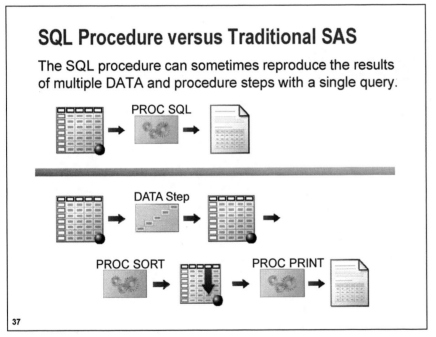

37

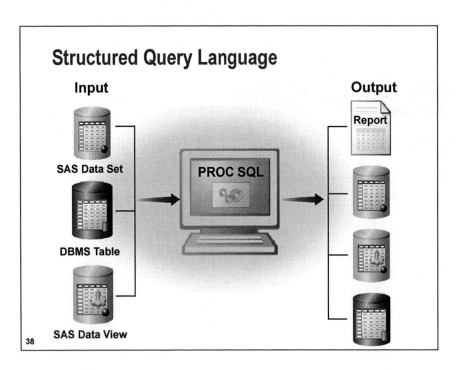

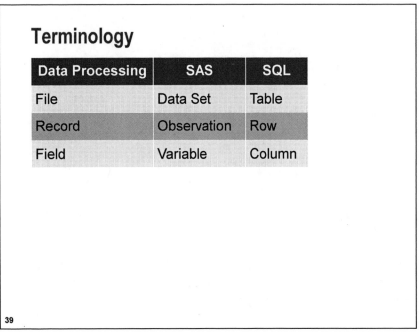

Chapter 2   Basic Queries

2.1 Overview of the SQL Procedure

Objectives

- Identify key syntax of the SQL procedure.
- List key features of the SQL procedure.
- List key features of the SELECT statement.
- List SQL procedure statements.

3

Business Scenario

As a new Orion Star programmer, you have inherited several SQL programs. You need to learn the PROC SQL syntax to use and extend these programs and ultimately write your own.

4

The SQL Procedure

The SQL procedure is initiated with a PROC SQL statement. It is terminated with a QUIT statement.

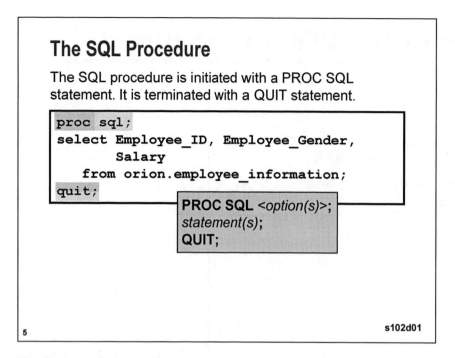

```
proc sql;
select Employee_ID, Employee_Gender,
       Salary
   from orion.employee_information;
quit;
```

PROC SQL <option(s)>;
statement(s);
QUIT;

5

s102d01

PROC SQL does not require a RUN statement. It uses the QUIT statement to explicitly terminate SQL processing. The SQL procedure, like other SAS procedures, is terminated if SAS encounters a DATA step or a PROC step.

SQL Procedure

- Multiple statements can be included in a PROC SQL step.
- Each statement defines a process and is executed immediately.

PROC SQL <option(s)>;
statement(s);
QUIT;

6

SELECT Statement

A *SELECT statement* is used to query one or more tables. The results of the SELECT statement are written to the default output destination.

```
proc sql;
select Employee_ID, Employee_Gender, Salary
   from orion.employee_information
   where Employee_Gender='F'
   order by Salary desc;
quit;
```

s102d01

7

SELECT Statement

A SELECT statement contains smaller building blocks called *clauses*.

```
proc sql;
select Employee_ID, Employee_Gender, Salary
   from orion.employee_information
   where Employee_Gender='F'
clauses  order by Salary desc;
quit;
```

✏ Although it can contain multiple clauses, each SELECT statement begins with the SELECT keyword and ends with a semicolon.

s102d01

8

Viewing the Output

Partial PROC SQL Output

```
                    The SAS System

                                       Employee
                         Employee        Annual
    Employee ID        Gender            Salary

        120260         F               $207,885
        120719         F                $87,420
        120661         F                $85,495
        121144         F                $83,505
        120798         F                $80,755
```

9

SELECT Statement: Required Clauses

> **SELECT** *object-item <, ...object-item>*
>   **FROM** *from-list*;

- The SELECT clause specifies the columns and column order.
- The FROM clause specifies the data sources.
- You can query from 1 to 256 tables.

10

SELECT Statement: Optional Clauses

```
SELECT object-item <, ...object-item>
    FROM from-list
    <WHERE sql-expression>
    <GROUP BY object-item <, ... object-item >>
    <HAVING sql-expression>
    <ORDER BY order-by-item <DESC>
            <, ...order-by-item>>
```

- The WHERE clause specifies data that meets certain conditions.
- The GROUP BY clause groups data for processing.
- The HAVING clause specifies groups that meet certain conditions.
- The ORDER BY clause specifies an order for the data.

11

SELECT Statement Syntax

```
PROC SQL;
SELECT object-item <, ...object-item>
    FROM from-list;
    <WHERE sql-expression>
    <GROUP BY object-item <, ... object-item >>
    <HAVING sql-expression>
    <ORDER BY order-by-item <DESC>
            <, ...order-by-item>>;
QUIT;
```

- ✎ The specified order of the above clauses within the SELECT statement is required.

12

Business Scenario

You have encountered a syntax error in one of the programs. What techniques exist to check the PROC SQL code for syntax errors?

13

Setup for the Poll

- Open and submit the program **s102a01**.
- View the SAS log.
- Consider the notes from the first two steps.
    1) Which step generated an error?
    2) What error message was generated?

14

2.01 Multiple Choice Poll

Which step generated an error?

a. Step 1
b. Step 2

s102a01

15

2.02 Quiz

What error message was generated in Step 2?

```
 /* Step 2 */
proc sql;
select Employee_ID, Employee_Gender,
       Salary
   from orion.employee_information
   order by EmpID
   where Employee_Gender='M';
quit;
```

s102a01

17

2.03 Quiz

- Open and submit the program **s102a02**.
- View the SAS output and log.

Did the code generate any output?

What does the note in the log indicate?

19   s102a02

Features of the VALIDATE Statement

```
proc sql;
validate
select Employee_ID, Employee_Gender,
       Salary
   from orion.employee_information
   where Employee_Gender='M'
   order by Employee_ID;
quit;
```

The VALIDATE statement

- is used only in conjunction with SELECT statements
- tests the syntax without executing the query
- checks table and column name validity
- prints error messages for invalid queries.

21

Viewing the Log

A common syntax error is to end a clause with a semicolon.

Partial SAS Log

```
39    proc sql;
40    validate
41    select Employee_ID, Employee_Gender,
42         Salary;
                  -
                  22
                  76
ERROR 22-322: Syntax error, expecting one of the following:
```

s102d02

22

NOEXEC Option

To explicitly check for syntax errors without submitting the code for execution, include the NOEXEC option in the PROC SQL statement. This option applies to all statements in a PROC SQL step.

PROC SQL <NOEXEC>;

```
proc sql noexec;
select Employee_ID, Employee_Gender, Salary
    from orion.employee_information
    where Employee_Gender='F'
    order by Salary desc;
quit;
```

s102d03

23

Viewing the Log

Partial SAS Log

```
proc sql noexec;
select Employee_ID, Employee_Gender, Salary
    from orion.employee_information
    where Employee_Gender='F'
    order by Salary desc;
NOTE: Statement not executed due to NOEXEC option.
quit;
```

24

Resetting Options

After an option is specified, it remains in effect for the PROC SQL step. You can use the RESET statement to add or change PROC SQL options without restarting the procedure.

RESET *option(s)*;

25

In a PROC SQL step, you can use options for many purposes. For details about available options, see the *SAS 9.3 SQL Procedure: User's Guide*.

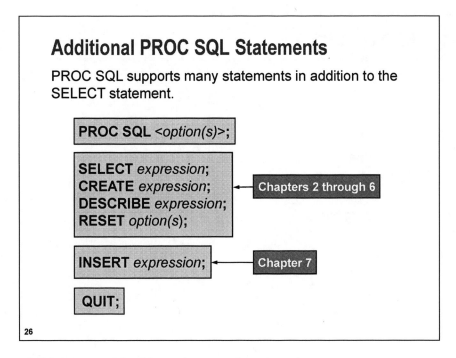

SELECT   identifies columns to be selected.

CREATE   builds new tables, views, or indexes.

DESCRIBE   displays table attributes or view definitions.

INSERT   adds rows of data to tables.

RESET   adds to or changes PROC SQL options without re-invoking the procedure.

2.2 Specifying Columns

Objectives

- Explore unfamiliar data.
- Display columns directly from a table.
- Display columns calculated from other columns in a query.
- Calculate columns conditionally using the CASE expression.
- Create a table from query results.

29

Business Scenario

Your manager has requested analysis of a table that is unfamiliar to you. You need to learn about the PROC SQL statements and options to explore the structure of the table and the data that it contains.

30

Querying All Columns in a Table

To print all of a table's columns in the order in which they were stored, specify an asterisk in a SELECT clause.

```
proc sql;
select *
    from orion.employee_information;
quit;
```

Partial PROC SQL Output

```
                              The SAS System
                Start
Employee ID      Date   End Date  Department
                         Employee              Employee               Employee
                          Annual  Employee       Birth    Employee  Termination  Manager for
Employee Job Title        Salary  Gender          Date   Hire Date      Date      Employee

      120101  01JUL2007  31DEC9999  Sales Management
Director                 $163,040  M            18AUG1980  01JUL2007       .        120261
```

s102d04

31

FEEDBACK Option

When using an asterisk in the SELECT clause, add the FEEDBACK option to write the expanded SELECT statement to the SAS log.

PROC SQL <option(s)>;

```
proc sql feedback;
select *
    from orion.employee_information;
quit;
```

32

Setup for the Poll

Submit the program **s102a03** and review the SAS log to answer the following question:

How are the column names represented in the expanded SELECT statement?

33

2.04 Multiple Choice Poll

How are the column names represented in the expanded SELECT statement?

a. The column names are preceded by the table name **EMPLOYEE_INFORMATION**.

b. The column names are preceded by the library reference **orion**.

c. The column names are preceded by the library reference **work**.

34

Viewing the Log

The column names are preceded by the table name.

Partial SAS Log

```
   proc sql feedback;
   select *
      from orion.employee_information;
NOTE: Statement transforms to:

        select EMPLOYEE_INFORMATION.Employee_ID,
EMPLOYEE_INFORMATION.Start_Date,EMPLOYEE_INFORMATION.End_Date,
EMPLOYEE_INFORMATION.Department, EMPLOYEE_INFORMATION.Job_Title,
EMPLOYEE_INFORMATION.Salary, EMPLOYEE_INFORMATION.Employee_Gender,
EMPLOYEE_INFORMATION.Birth_Date,EMPLOYEE_INFORMATION.Employee_Hire_Date,
EMPLOYEE_INFORMATION.Employee_Term_Date,EMPLOYEE_INFORMATION.Manager_ID
          from ORION.EMPLOYEE_INFORMATION;

   quit;
```

36

s102a03

DESCRIBE Statement

Use the DESCRIBE statement to see the table's column names and their attributes in the SAS log.

DESCRIBE TABLE|VIEW *table-name*;

```
proc sql;
describe table orion.employee_information;
quit;
```

Partial SAS Log

```
Employee_ID num format=12. label='Employee ID',
Start_Date num format=DATE9. label='Start Date',
End_Date num format=DATE9. label='End Date',
Department char(40),
Job_Title char(25) label='Employee Job Title',
Salary num format=DOLLAR12. label='Employee Annual Salary',
Employee_Gender char(1) label='Employee Gender',
Birth_Date num format=DATE9. label='Employee Birth Date',
Employee_Hire_Date num format=DATE9. informat=DATE9.,
Employee_Term_Date num format=DATE9. informat=DATE9.,
```

37

s102d05

Business Scenario

Produce a report that contains selected information for all Orion Star employees.

orion.employee_information

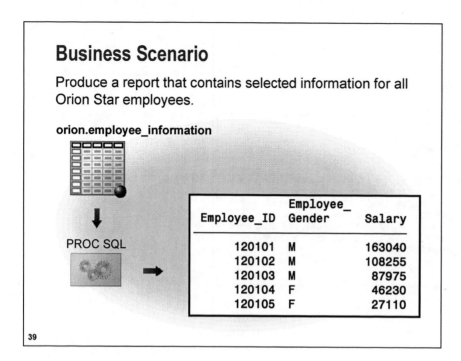

Employee_ID	Employee_Gender	Salary
120101	M	163040
120102	M	108255
120103	M	87975
120104	F	46230
120105	F	27110

39

Querying Specific Columns in a Table

List the columns that you want and the order to display them in the SELECT clause.

```
proc sql;
select Employee_ID, Employee_Gender,
       Salary
   from orion.employee_information;
quit;
```

40   s102d06

✎   Remember to use commas to separate items in a list, such as a list of column names in the SELECT, GROUP BY, or ORDER BY clauses.

Viewing the Output

Partial PROC SQL Output

```
              The SAS System

                                     Employee
                        Employee       Annual
   Employee ID  Gender               Salary

        120101  M                   $163,040
        120102  M                   $108,255
        120103  M                    $87,975
        120104  F                    $46,230
        120105  F                    $27,110
        120106  M                    $26,960
        120107  F                    $30,475
```

41

2.05 Quiz

Submit the program **s102a04** and review the SAS log to answer the following question:

What syntax error was identified in the log?

42

Business Scenario

Modify the previous report by creating a new column, **Bonus,** which contains an amount equal to 10% of the employee's salary.

orion.employee_information

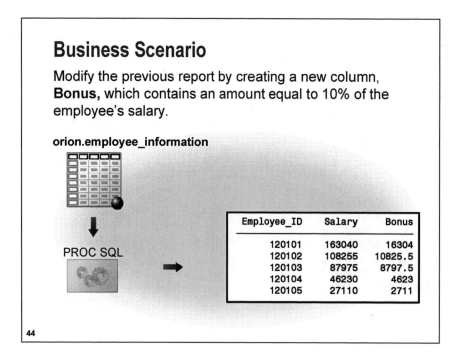

Employee_ID	Salary	Bonus
120101	163040	16304
120102	108255	10825.5
120103	87975	8797.5
120104	46230	4623
120105	27110	2711

44

Calculated Columns

Name the new column using the AS keyword.

```
proc sql;
select Employee_ID, Salary,
       Salary*.10 as Bonus
   from orion.employee_information;
quit;
```

Partial PROC SQL Output

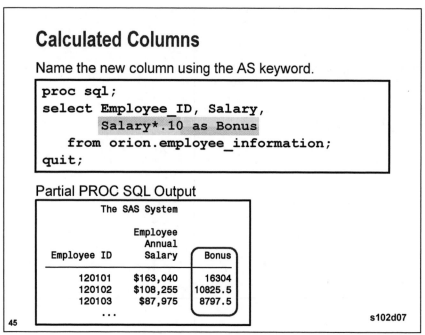

45   s102d07

✎ The new column name, **Bonus**, is called an *alias*. Assigning an alias to a calculated column is optional, but if an alias *is* assigned, the AS keyword is required. Omission of the alias causes the column heading in the report to be blank.

Business Scenario

You have been asked to modify the previous bonus report to conditionally calculate bonuses.

Job Title Level	Bonus Percent
I	5%
II	7%
III	10%
IV	12%
Other	8%

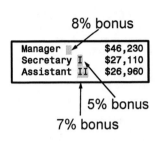

8% bonus

```
Manager       $46,230
Secretary I   $27,110
Assistant II  $26,960
```

5% bonus

7% bonus

46

2.06 Multiple Choice Poll

Which of these SAS character functions is the most useful for identifying the level value for conditional processing?

a. CHAR( )
b. FIND( )
c. SCAN( )
d. SUBSTR( )

47

SCAN Function

The *SCAN function* returns the *n*th word or segment from a character string after breaking it up by the delimiters.

scan(Job_Title,3,' ')		Office Assistant III

SCAN(*string,count<,charlist><,modifier(s)>*)

string	a character constant, variable, or expression
count	an integer specifying the number of the word or segment that you want SCAN to select
charlist	characters used as delimiters to separate words
modifier	a character that modifies the action of the SCAN function

49

If the third argument (*charlist*) is omitted, the default delimiters are as shown below:

ASCII (PC, UNIX)	blank . < (+ | & ! $ *) ; - / , % ^
EBCDIC (z/0s)	blank . < (+ | & ! $ *) ; - / , % ¢ ¬

The two most commonly use modifiers are I and T.

I – indicates to ignore the case of the characters.

T – indicates to trim trailing blanks from the *string* and *charlist* arguments.

Extracting the Level from Job_Title

Return the third word from **Job_Title** using a blank space as the delimiter. The SCAN function processes from left to right when the value of the count argument is positive.

scan(Job_Title,3,' ')

50   ...

Extracting the Level from Job_Title

Some **Job_Title** values have fewer than three words. If the value of *count* is greater than the number of words in the character string, the SCAN function returns a missing value.

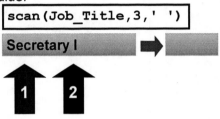

51

...

Extracting the Level from Job_Title

The SCAN function processes from right to left when the value of the *count* argument is negative.

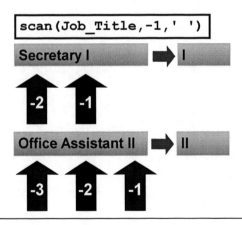

52

CASE Expression

To create new columns conditionally, use the CASE
expression in the SELECT list.

```
SELECT object-item<, ...object-item>,
       CASE <case-operand>
         WHEN when-condition THEN result-expression
         <WHEN when-condition THEN result-expression>
         <ELSE result-expression>
         END <AS column>
       FROM table;
```

There are two forms of the CASE expression.

The CASE expression is evaluated for each row of a table
and returns a single value.

53

Calculating Columns Conditionally: CASE

CASE Expression: Standard Form

```
select Job_Title, Salary,
       case
          when scan(Job_Title,-1,' ')='I'
              then Salary*.05
          when scan(Job_Title,-1,' ')='II'
              then Salary*.07
          when scan(Job_Title,-1,' ')='III'
              then Salary*.10
          when scan(Job_Title,-1,' ')='IV'
              then Salary*.12
          else Salary*.08
       end as Bonus
    from orion.employee_information;
```

With this form of the CASE syntax, you can use equality
and non-equality tests for validity.

54   s102d08

Calculating Columns Conditionally: CASE

CASE Expression: Standard Form

```
select Job_Title, Salary,
       case
           when scan(Job_Title,-1,' ')='I'
               then Salary*.05
           when scan(Job_Title,-1,' ')='II'
               then Salary*.07
           when scan(Job_Title,-1,' ')='III'
               then Salary*.10
           when scan(Job_Title,-1,' ')='IV'
               then Salary*.12
           else Salary*.08
       end as Bon
   from orion.emp
```

> The first WHEN clause evaluated as true determines which value the CASE expression returns. Subsequent WHEN clauses are not evaluated.

s102d08

55

Calculating Columns Conditionally: CASE

CASE Expression: Standard Form

```
select Job_Title, Salary,
       case
           when scan(Job_
               then Sala
           when scan(Job_
               then Sala
           when scan(Job_
               then Sala
           when scan(Job_
               then Salary*.12
           else Salary*.08
       end as Bonus
   from orion.employee_information;
```

> The optional ELSE expression provides an alternate action if none of the WHEN expressions are true.
>
> If no ELSE expression is present and every WHEN condition is false, the CASE expression returns a missing value.

s102d08

56

Calculating Columns Conditionally: CASE

CASE Expression: Shortcut (Case-Operand) Form

```
select Job_Title, Salary,                    Case
       case scan(Job_Title,-1,' ')           operand
            when 'I' then Salary*.05
            when 'II' then Salary*.07
            when 'III' then Salary*.10
            when 'IV' then Salary*.12
            else Salary*.08
       end as Bonus
    from orion.employee_information;
```

> ✏ With this form of the CASE syntax, you can use only an equality test for validity.

s102d08

57

> ✏ The shortcut form is more efficient because the SCAN function is evaluated only once, but this method requires an EQUAL comparison operator. If you need a different operator, use the standard form.

Viewing the Output

Partial PROC SQL Output

```
                        The SAS System

                              Employee
                                Annual
        Employee Job Title      Salary      Bonus


        Director              $163,040    13043.2
        Sales Manager         $108,255     8660.4
        Sales Manager          $87,975       7038
        Administration Manager $46,230     3698.4
        Secretary I            $27,110     1355.5
        Office Assistant II    $26,960     1887.2
        Office Assistant III   $30,475     3047.5
        Warehouse Assistant II $27,660     1936.2
        Warehouse Assistant I  $26,495    1324.75
```

58

Business Scenario

Management needs a report that includes the employee identifier, gender, and age for an upcoming audit.

Here is a sketch of the desired report:

Employee_ID	Employee_Gender	Age
120101	M	32
120102	M	39

59

Business Data

Employee data is stored in the **orion.employee_information** table. An employee's age can be calculated based on his or her birthdate.

orion.employee_information

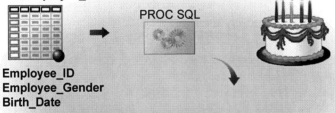

Employee_ID
Employee_Gender
Birth_Date

Employee_ID	Employee_Gender	Age
120101	M	32
120102	M	39

60

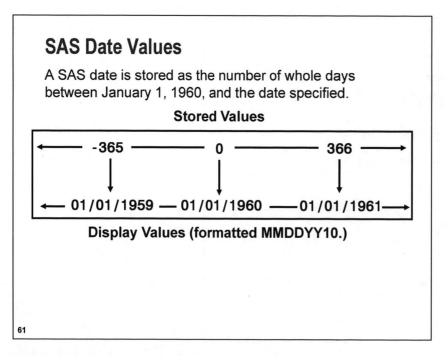

SAS date constants are used throughout this course.

Syntax	Used to	Example
'ddMONyyyy'd	Convert a calendar date into a SAS date value	'15JUN2008'd as Date

Selected SAS Numeric Functions

The following SAS numeric functions are frequently used when you work with SAS dates.

Function	Used To Return	Example
TODAY()	Today's date as a SAS date value (integer)	`today() as Date`
MONTH(arg)	The month portion of a SAS date variable as an integer between 1-12	`month(Birth_Date) as Birth_Month`
INT(arg)	The integer portion of a numeric value	`int(fullage) as Age`

62

PROC SQL supports most SAS DATA step functions. However, some are not supported (for example, the LAG and DIF functions). For a complete list of functions that are not supported in SQL, see the most recent documentation.

Calculating Columns Using SAS Dates: Step 1

Calculate **Age** based on today's date being 02JAN2013 and a **Birth_Date** value of 18AUG1980.

```
                    19360                    7535
proc sql;
select Employee_ID, Employee_Gender,
       int((today()-Birth_Date)/365.25)
       as Age
   from orion.employee_information;
quit;
```

s102d09

63

Calculating Columns Using SAS Dates: Step 2

Calculate **Age** based on today's date being 02JAN2013 and a **Birth_Date** value of 18AUG1980.

```
proc sql;
select Employee_ID, Employee_Gender,
       int((today()-Birth_Date)/365.25)
       as Age
   from orion.employee_information;    32.3751
quit;
```

s102d09

64

Calculating Columns Using SAS Dates: Step 3

Calculate **Age** based on today's date being 02JAN2013 and a **Birth_Date** value of 18AUG1980.

```
proc sql;
select Employee_ID, Employee_Gender,
   32  int((today()-Birth_Date)/365.25)
      as Age
   from orion.employee_information;
quit;
```

65   s102d09

Viewing the Output

Partial PROC SQL Output

```
              The SAS System

              Employee
Employee ID   Gender           Age

   120101    M                 32
   120102    M                 39
   120103    M                 59
   120104    F                 54
   120105    F                 34
   120106    M                 64
   120107    F                 59
```

The values of **Age** vary based on the date that the program is executed.

66

2.07 Quiz

What date function would you use to create the **Birth_Month** column for the following rows from the **employee_information** table?

```
                         The SAS System

                                                   Employee_
  Employee_ID   Birth_Date   Birth_Month           Gender

       120101         7535             8            M
       120102         4971             8            M
       120103        -2535             1            M
       120104         -600             5            F
       120105         6929            12            F
       120106        -4026            12            M
       120107        -2536             1            F
```

67

Business Scenario

To support management's requests for reports, you need to create a new table that contains selected columns from an existing table and a calculated column named **Birth_Month**.

orion.employee_information   PROC SQL   work.birth_months

69

Creating and Populating a Table

To define the structure of the **work.birth_months** table, use the SELECT list.

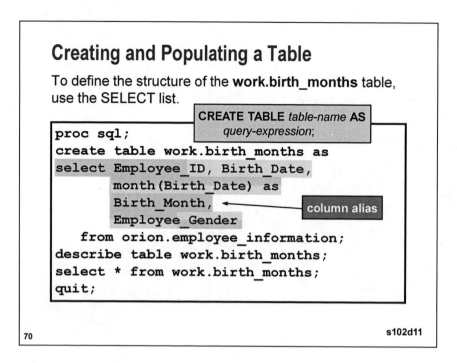

```
proc sql;
create table work.birth_months as
select Employee_ID, Birth_Date,
       month(Birth_Date) as
       Birth_Month,
       Employee_Gender
   from orion.employee_information;
describe table work.birth_months;
select * from work.birth_months;
quit;
```

CREATE TABLE *table-name* AS
query-expression;

column alias

70   s102d11

If a new column is computed, the column name in the new table is the name of the alias.

If a table is created and an alias is not assigned, the omission of the AS keyword causes the new column name to be **_TEMA001**. If other new columns are created without the AS keyword, the new names would be **_TEMA002**, **_TEMA003**, and so on.

Viewing the Log

Partial SAS Log

```
121   proc sql;
122   create table work.birth_months as
123   select Employee_ID,  Birth_Date,
124          month(Birth_Date) as Birth_Month,
125          Employee_Gender
126      from orion.employee_information;
NOTE: Table WORK.BIRTH_MONTHS created, with 424 rows and 4 columns.

127   describe table work.birth_months;
NOTE: SQL table WORK.BIRTH_MONTHS was created like:

create table WORK.BIRTH_MONTHS( bufsize=4096 )
   (
   Employee_ID num format=12.,
   Birth_Date num,
   Birth_Month num,
   Employee_Gender char(1)
   );
```

71

Viewing the Output

Partial PROC SQL Output

```
                        The SAS System

                                         Employee_
 Employee_ID  Birth_Date  Birth_Month    Gender

     120101       7535            8       M
     120102       4971            8       M
     120103      -2535            1       M
     120104       -600            5       F
     120105       6929           12       F
     120106      -4026           12       M
     120107      -2536            1       F
```

72

Exercises

If you restarted your SAS session since the last exercise, open and submit the **libname.sas** program found in the data folder.

Level 1

1. **Querying a Table**

   a. Write a query that displays all rows and all columns from the **orion.employee_payroll** table.

   Partial PROC SQL Output

Employee_ID	Employee_Gender	Salary	Birth_Date	Employee_Hire_Date	Employee_Term_Date	Marital_Status	Dependents
120101	M	163040	7535	17384	.	S	0
120102	M	108255	4971	12205	.	O	2
120103	M	87975	-2535	6575	.	M	1
120104	F	46230	-600	9132	.	M	1
120105	F	27110	6929	15826	.	S	0

   b. Modify the previous query so that only the columns for **Employee_ID**, **Employee_Gender**, **Marital_Status**, and **Salary** are displayed.

Partial PROC SQL Output

Employee_ID	Employee_ Gender	Marital_ Status	Salary
120101	M	S	163040
120102	M	O	108255
120103	M	M	87975
120104	F	M	46230
120105	F	S	27110

Level 2

2. Calculating a Column

Write a query that generates the report below. The report should do the following:

- display **Employee_ID**, **Employee_Gender**, **Marital_Status**, **Salary**, and a new column (**Tax**) that is one-third of the employee's salary
- use the **orion.employee_payroll** table

Partial PROC SQL Output

Employee_ID	Employee_ Gender	Marital_ Status	Salary	Tax
120101	M	S	163040	54346.67
120102	M	O	108255	36085
120103	M	M	87975	29325
120104	F	M	46230	15410
120105	F	S	27110	9036.667
120106	M	M	26960	8986.667

3. Creating a New Table

Create a new table named **work.bonus**.

- The new table should include these columns: **Employee_ID**, **Salary**, a new column representing a 4% bonus (**Bonus**).
- Use the **orion.employee_payroll** table as the basis.
- In the same SQL step, generate a report of the new table.

SAS Log Output

```
NOTE: Table WORK.BONUS created, with 424 rows and 3 columns.
```

Partial PROC SQL Output

Employee_ID	Salary	Bonus
120101	163040	6521.6
120102	108255	4330.2
120103	87975	3519
120104	46230	1849.2
120105	27110	1084.4
120106	26960	1078.4

Challenge

4. **Conditional Processing**

    Create a report that displays **Employee_ID**, **Level**, **Salary**, and **Salary_Range** using the **orion.staff** table. **Level** and **Salary_Range** are two new columns in the report. The report should also contain salary information for only the Orion Star executives. Conditionally, assign values to the two new columns as follows:

Job_Title (Last Word)	Level	Salary Ranges		
		Low	Medium	High
Manager	Manager	< 52,000	52,000-72,000	> 72,000
Director	Director	<108,000	108,000-135,000	> 135,000
Officer, President	Executive	<240,000	240,000-300,000	> 300,000
Other	N/A	DO NOT INCLUDE IN THE REPORT.		

    Partial PROC SQL Output

    ```
                                       Employee
                                         Annual
                  Employee ID  Level     Salary  Salary_Range
                  _____

                       120101  Director $163,040  High
                       120659  Director $161,290  High
                       121142  Director $156,065  High
                       120800  Director  $80,210  Low
                       120270  Director  $48,435  Low
                       120259  Executive $433,800  High
    ```

    Why are you seeing column headings instead of column names in your output?

2.3 Specifying Rows

Objectives

- Eliminate duplicate rows in a query.
- Select a subset of rows in a query.

76

Business Scenario

Display the names of the Orion Star departments using the **orion.employee_information** table.

Desired Report

```
               The SAS System

Department
_____

Accounts
Accounts Management
Administration
Concession Management
...
```

No duplicates should appear in the report.

77

Displaying All Rows

```
proc sql;
select Department
    from orion.employee_information;
quit;
```

Partial PROC SQL Output

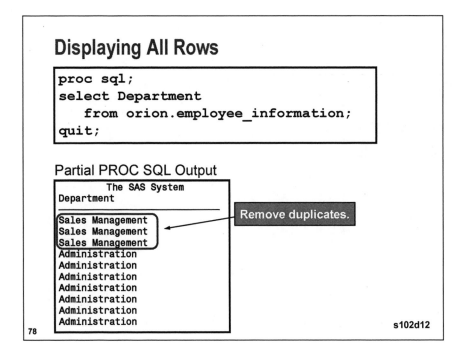

s102d12

78

Eliminating Duplicate Rows

Use the *DISTINCT* keyword to eliminate duplicate rows.

```
proc sql;
select distinct Department
    from orion.employee_information;
quit;
```

✎   The DISTINCT keyword applies to all columns in the SELECT list. One row is displayed for each unique combination of values.

79

s102d13

✎   UNIQUE is an alternative keyword for DISTINCT. It is a SAS enhancement.

Viewing the Output

Partial PROC SQL Output

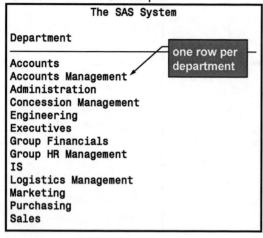

```
                    The SAS System

Department
──────────────────────
Accounts
Accounts Management
Administration
Concession Management
Engineering
Executives
Group Financials
Group HR Management
IS
Logistics Management
Marketing
Purchasing
Sales
```

one row per department

80

2.08 Multiple Choice Poll

Which partial SELECT statement selects only the unique combinations of **Employee_Gender** and **Job_Title**?

a. `select distinct Employee_Gender,`
   `distinct Job_Title...`

b. `select distinct Employee_Gender,`
   `Job_Title...`

c. `select distinct Employee_Gender`
   `Job_Title...`

81

Business Scenario

Management requested a list of employees whose salaries exceed $112,000.

orion.employee_information

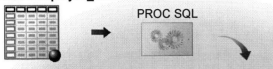

PROC SQL

Employee ID	Employee Job Title	Employee Annual Salary
120101	Director	$163,040
120259	Chief Executive Officer	$433,800
120260	Chief Marketing Officer	$207,885
120261	Chief Sales Officer	$243,190
120262	Chief Financial Officer	$268,455

83

Subsetting with the WHERE Clause

Use a WHERE clause to specify a condition that the data must satisfy before being selected.

```
proc sql;
select Employee_ID, Job_Title, Salary
   from orion.employee_information
   where Salary > 112000;
quit;
```

WHERE *sql-expression*

84   s102d14

Viewing the Output

PROC SQL Output

```
                          The SAS System
                                                    Employee
                                                      Annual
      Employee ID  Employee Job Title                 Salary


             120101   Director                       $163,040
             120259   Chief Executive Officer        $433,800
             120260   Chief Marketing Officer        $207,885
             120261   Chief Sales Officer            $243,190
             120262   Chief Financial Officer        $268,455
             120659   Director                       $161,290
             121141   Vice President                 $194,885
             121142   Director                       $156,065
```

85

Subsetting: Comparison Operators

You can use all common comparison operators in a WHERE clause.

Mnemonic	Symbol	Definition
LT †	<	Less than
GT †	>	Greater than
EQ †	=	Equal to
LE †	<=	Less than or equal to
GE †	>=	Greater than or equal to
NE †	< >	Not equal to
	¬= †	Not equal to (EBCDIC)
	^= †	Not equal to (ASCII)

86

† SAS enhancement

Subsetting: Logical Operators

Use only one WHERE clause in a SELECT statement. To specify multiple subsetting criteria, combine expressions with logical operators.

Mnemonic	Symbol	Definition
OR	| †	or, either
AND	& †	and, both
NOT	¬ †	not, negation (EBCDIC)
NOT	^ †	not, negation (ASCII)

87

† SAS enhancement

Subsetting: Special Operators

Common WHERE clause operators with examples:

Operator	Example
IN	where JobCategory in ('PT','NA','FA')
CONTAINS or ? †	where word ? 'LAM'
IS NULL or IS MISSING †	where Product_ID is missing
BETWEEN – AND	where Salary between 70000 and 80000
SOUNDS LIKE (=*) †	where LastName =* 'SMITH'
LIKE using % or _	where Employee_Name like 'H%' where JobCategory like '__1'

88

† SAS enhancement

Alternative statements for using the IS NULL or IS MISSING operator are as follows:

- **where Product_ID = ' '**
- **where Product_ID = .**

With the = operator, you must know whether **Product_ID** is character or numeric. However, if you use IS MISSING or IS NULL, you do not need advance knowledge of the column type.

2.09 Quiz

Modify program **s102a05** to provide a WHERE expression that selects only those rows in which the employees' first names begin with N.

Desired PROC SQL Output

The SAS System	
Employee_Name	Employee_ID
Apr, Nishan	120759
James, Narelle	120155
Kokoszka, Nikeisha	120765
Plybon, Nicholas	120276
Post, Nahliah	120748
Smith, Nasim	121032

89

Business Scenario

Management requested a report that includes only those employees who receive bonuses less than $3000.

orion.employee_information

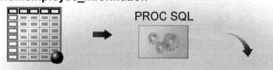

PROC SQL

Employee_ID	Employee_ Gender	Salary	Bonus
120105	F	27110	2711
120106	M	26960	2696
120108	F	27660	2766
120109	F	26495	2649.5
120110	M	28615	2861.5

91

Subsetting with Calculated Values

First attempt:

```
proc sql;
select Employee_ID, Employee_Gender,
       Salary, Salary*.10 as Bonus
  from orion.employee_information
  where Bonus<3000;
quit;
```

A *WHERE* clause is evaluated before the *SELECT* clause. Therefore, columns used in the WHERE clause must exist in the table.

Partial SAS Log

```
ERROR: The following columns were not found in the contributing
tables: Bonus.
```

s102d15

92

Subsetting with Calculated Values

One solution is to repeat the calculation in the WHERE clause.

```
proc sql;
select Employee_ID, Employee_Gender,
       Salary, Salary*.10 as Bonus
  from orion.employee_information
  where Salary*.10<3000;
quit;
```

ANSI standard

s102d15

93

Subsetting with Calculated Values

An alternate method is to use the CALCULATED keyword in the WHERE clause.

```
proc sql;
select Employee_ID, Employee_Gender,
       Salary, Salary*.10 as Bonus
   from orion.employee_information
   where calculated Bonus<3000;
quit;
```

SAS enhancement

94   s102d15

Viewing the Output

Partial PROC SQL Output

```
                        The SAS System

                                    Employee
                        Employee      Annual
            Employee ID  Gender        Salary      Bonus
            ─────────────────────────────────────────────
               120105    F           $27,110       2711
               120106    M           $26,960       2696
               120108    F           $27,660       2766
               120109    F           $26,495      2649.5
               120110    M           $28,615      2861.5
               120111    M           $26,895      2689.5
               120112    F           $26,550       2655
```

95

Using the Calculated Keyword

You can also use the CALCULATED keyword in other parts of a query.

```
proc sql;
select Employee_ID, Employee_Gender,
       Salary, Salary*.10 as Bonus,
       calculated Bonus/2 as Half
   from orion.employee_information
   where calculated Bonus<3000;
quit;
```

s102d15

96

The CALCULATED keyword or repeated calculated column expression is required when referring to any calculated column, character or numeric, in the SELECT or WHERE clause, but it is not necessary with the ORDER BY or HAVING clause.

Example:

```
select Employee_ID, Salary,
       (scan(Job_Title,-1,' ')) as Job_Level
   from orion.Staff
   where calculated Job_Level='IV';
```

Viewing the Output

Partial PROC SQL Output

The SAS System

Employee ID	Employee Gender	Employee Annual Salary	Bonus	Half
120105	F	$27,110	2711	1355.5
120106	M	$26,960	2696	1348
120108	F	$27,660	2766	1383
120109	F	$26,495	2649.5	1324.75
120110	M	$28,615	2861.5	1430.75
120111	M	$26,895	2689.5	1344.75
120112	F	$26,550	2655	1327.5

97

Exercises

> If you restarted your SAS session since the last exercise, open and submit the **libname.sas** program found in the data folder.

Level 1

5. Eliminating Duplicates

Write a query that generates a report that displays the cities where the Orion Star employees reside. The report should do the following:

- display one unique row per **City**
- use the **orion.employee_addresses** table

PROC SQL Output

```
                              City
                              _____

                              Melbourne
                              Miami-Dade
                              Philadelphia
                              San Diego
                              Sydney
```

Level 2

6. Subsetting Data

Write a query that generates a report that displays Orion Star employees whose charitable contributions exceed $90.00. The report should have the following characteristics:

- display **Employee_ID**, **Recipients**, and the new column **Total** that represents the total charitable contribution for each employee over the four quarters
- use the **orion.employee_donations** table
- include only employees whose charitable contribution **Total** for all four quarters exceeds $90.00

Hint: The total charitable contribution is calculated by adding the amount of **Qtr1**, **Qtr2**, **Qtr3**, and **Qtr4**. Use the SUM function to ensure that missing values are ignored.

Partial PROC SQL Output

Employee ID	Recipients	Total
120660	Disaster Assist, Inc.	100
120677	EarthSalvors 60%, Vox Victimas 40%	100
120753	Conserve Nature, Inc. 50%, AquaMissions International 50%	100
120766	Mitleid International 80%, Save the Baby Animals 20%	100
120791	Child Survivors	120

Challenge

7. **Subsetting Data Using the ESCAPE Clause**

   Create a report that displays the **Employee_ID** and **Recipients** for all employees who contributed 90% of their charitable contributions to a single company that was incorporated (Inc.) and is the last recipient in the list to receive the 90% contribution. Use the **orion.employee_donations** table.

   Hint: Use the ESCAPE clause in the WHERE clause to solve this problem.

    Alternative methods can be used to solve this problem, but for this exercise, use the LIKE operator with an ESCAPE clause.

   PROC SQL Output

Employee ID	Recipients
120783	Disaster Assist, Inc. 10%, Cancer Cures, Inc. 90%
121012	Child Survivors 10%, Disaster Assist, Inc. 90%
121136	Disaster Assist, Inc. 10%, Cancer Cures, Inc. 90%

2.4 Solutions

Solutions to Exercises

1. **Querying a Table**

   a.
   ```
   *** s102s01 ***;
   proc sql;
   select *
      from orion.employee_payroll;
   quit;
   ```

   b.
   ```
   proc sql;
   select Employee_ID, Employee_Gender, Marital_Status, Salary
      from orion.employee_payroll;
   quit;
   ```

2. **Calculating a Column**
   ```
   *** s102s02 ***;
   proc sql;
   select Employee_ID, Employee_Gender, Marital_Status,
          Salary, Salary/3 as Tax
      from orion.employee_payroll;
   quit;
   ```

3. **Creating a New Table**
   ```
   *** s102s03 ***;
   proc sql;
   create table work.bonus as
   ```

```
select Employee_ID, Salary,
       Salary * .04 as Bonus
   from orion.employee_payroll;
select * from work.bonus;
quit;
```

4. Conditional Processing

```
*** s102s04 ***;
proc sql;
select Employee_ID,
       case (scan(Job_Title,-1," "))
          when "Manager" then "Manager"
          when "Director" then "Director"
          when "Officer" then "Executive"
          when "President" then "Executive"
          else "N/A"
       end as Level,
       Salary,
       case (calculated Level)
          when "Manager" then
             case
                when (Salary>72000) then "High"
                when (Salary>52000) then "Medium"
                else "Low"
             end
          when "Director" then
             case
                when (Salary>135000) then "High"
                when (Salary>108000) then "Medium"
                else "Low"
             end
          when "Executive" then
             case
                when (Salary>300000) then "High"
                when (Salary>240000) then "Medium"
                else "Low"
             end
          else "N/A"
       end as Salary_Range
   from orion.Staff
   where calculated level ne "N/A"
   order by Level, Salary desc;
quit;
```

Why are you seeing column headings instead of column names in your output?

The label attribute is associated with these columns in the descriptor portion of the input SAS data set.

These labels are automatically used by PROC SQL.

5. Eliminating Duplicates

```
*** s102s05 ***;
proc sql;
select distinct City
   from orion.employee_addresses;
quit;
```

6. **Subsetting Data**

```
*** s102s06 ***;
proc sql;
select Employee_ID, Recipients,
       sum(Qtr1,Qtr2,Qtr3,Qtr4) as Total
   from orion.employee_donations
   where calculated Total>90;
quit;
```

7. **Subsetting Data Using the ESCAPE Clause**

```
*** s102s07 ***;
proc sql;
select Employee_ID, Recipients
   from orion.employee_donations
   where Recipients like "% Inc. 90~%" ESCAPE "~";
quit;
```

Solutions to Student Activities (Polls/Quizzes)

2.01 Multiple Choice Poll – Correct Answer

Which step generated an error?

a. Step 1
(b.) Step 2

16   s102a01

2.02 Quiz – Correct Answer

What error message was generated in Step 2?

```
 /* Step 2 */
proc sql;
select Employee_ID, Employee_Gender,
       Salary
   from orion.employee_information
   order by EmpID
➡ where Employee_Gender='M';
quit;
```

ERROR: Syntax error, expecting one of the following….

18   s102a01

2.03 Quiz – Correct Answer

Did the code generate any output?

no

What does the note in the log indicate?

Valid syntax – the VALIDATE statement checks the SELECT statement syntax.

Partial SAS Log

```
proc sql;
validate
select Employee_ID, Employee_Gender,
       Salary
   from orion.employee_information
   where Employee_Gender='M'
   order by Employee_ID;
NOTE: PROC SQL statement has valid syntax.
```

20   s102a02

2.04 Multiple Choice Poll – Correct Answer

How are the column names represented in the expanded SELECT statement?

(a.) The column names are preceded by the table name **EMPLOYEE_INFORMATION**.

b. The column names are preceded by the library reference **orion**.

c. The column names are preceded by the library reference **work**.

35

2.05 Quiz – Correct Answer

What syntax error was identified in the log?

Syntax error, expecting one of the following: ….

The commas used to separate the items in a list were omitted.

✎ Remember to use commas to separate items in a list, such as a list of column names in the SELECT, GROUP BY, or ORDER BY clauses.

43

2.06 Multiple Choice Poll – Correct Answer

Which of these SAS character functions is the most useful
for identifying the level value for conditional processing?

a. CHAR( )
b. FIND( )
c. SCAN( )
d. SUBSTR( )

48

2.07 Quiz – Correct Answer

What date function would you use to create the
Birth_Month column for the following rows from
the **employee_information** table?

the MONTH function

```
proc sql;
select Employee_ID, Birth_Date,
       month(Birth_Date) as Birth_Month,
       Employee_Gender
   from orion.employee_information;
quit;
```

68   s102d10

2.08 Multiple Choice Poll – Correct Answer

Which partial SELECT statement selects only the unique combinations of **Employee_Gender** and **Job_Title**?

a. `select distinct Employee_Gender,`
   `distinct Job_Title...`

b. `select distinct Employee_Gender,`
   `Job_Title...`

c. `select distinct Employee_Gender`
   `Job_Title...`

82

2.09 Quiz – Correct Answer

Modify program **s102a05** to provide a WHERE expression that selects only those rows in which the employees' first names begin with N.

One possible solution:

```
select Employee_Name, Employee_ID
   from orion.employee_addresses
   where Employee_Name contains ', N';
```

90   s102a05s

Chapter 3   Displaying Query Results

3.1 Presenting Data

Objectives

- Display a query's results in a specified order.
- Use SAS formats, labels, and titles to enhance the appearance and usability of a query's output.
- Use PROC SQL options to control the query's output.

3

Business Scenario

Management wants to analyze employee donation information. They requested two reports.

Report 1: first quarter donations in descending order

Employee ID	Qtr1
121143	35
121142	35
121145	35
120791	30
...	

Report 2: maximum quarterly donations in descending order with employee IDs in ascending order

Employee ID	
120265	25
120736	25
120270	20
120679	20
...	

4

Ordering Rows

Report 1: Use the ORDER BY clause to order the query results.

```
proc sql;
select Employee_ID, Qtr1
    from orion.employee_donations
    order by Qtr1 desc;
quit;
```

ORDER BY *order-by-item* <DESC>
     <,...*order-by-item* <DESC>>

The default sort order when using an ORDER BY clause is ascending (no keyword or **ASC**). Use the **DESC** keyword following the column name to reverse the order.

s103d01

5

The order of your output is guaranteed only if you include an ORDER BY clause in your query and the order is only guaranteed for the columns specified in the ORDER BY clause.

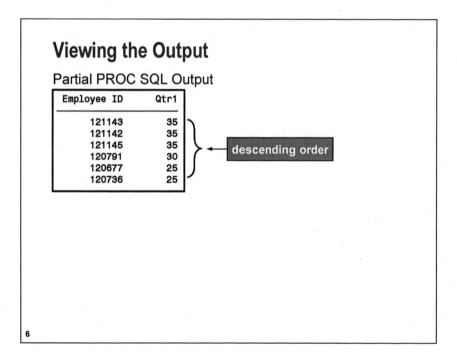

Viewing the Output

Partial PROC SQL Output

Employee ID	Qtr1
121143	35
121142	35
121145	35
120791	30
120677	25
120736	25

descending order

6

Ordering Rows

In an ORDER BY clause, *order-by-item* is one of the following:

> **ORDER BY** *order-by-item* **<DESC>**
> <,... *order-by-item* **<DESC>>**

- a column name from any table in the FROM clause, even if the column is not in the SELECT clause
- a column alias
- an integer representing the position of an item in the SELECT clause
- an sql-expression

If more than one *order-by-item* is specified, then the first one determines the major sort order.

7

3.01 Multiple Choice Poll

Which ORDER BY clause orders a report by descending **State** and descending **City**?

```
a.   order by desc State, City
b.   order by State, City desc
c.   order by State desc, City desc
d.   order by desc State, desc City
```

8

Ordering Rows

Report 2: Order the results in descending order of maximum quarterly donation and then by employee ID in ascending order.

```
proc sql;
select Employee_ID,
       max(Qtr1,Qtr2,Qtr3,Qtr4)
    from orion.employee_donations
    where Paid_By="Cash or Check"
    order by 2 desc, Employee_ID;
quit;
```

Mix and match!

s103d02

10

Viewing the Output

Partial PROC SQL Output

Employee ID	
120265	25
120736	25
120270	20
120679	20
120759	20
120760	20
120681	15
120734	15

ascending Employee_ID

descending donation amounts

11

Business Scenario

Enhance the previous report by adding descriptive
headings, displaying the donation column with dollar signs,
adding titles and constant text, and by numbering the rows.

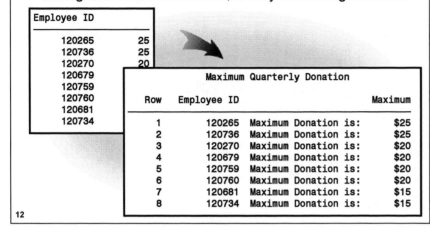

```
Employee ID

     120265       25
     120736       25
     120270       20
     120679
     120759
     120760
     120681
     120734
```

```
                 Maximum Quarterly Donation

    Row   Employee ID                            Maximum

      1       120265   Maximum Donation is:         $25
      2       120736   Maximum Donation is:         $25
      3       120270   Maximum Donation is:         $20
      4       120679   Maximum Donation is:         $20
      5       120759   Maximum Donation is:         $20
      6       120760   Maximum Donation is:         $20
      7       120681   Maximum Donation is:         $15
      8       120734   Maximum Donation is:         $15
```

12

Adding Formats and Column Labels

Column labels and formats must follow the column name
and precede the comma.

ANSI standard

```
proc sql;
select Employee_ID 'Employee ID',
       max(Qtr1,Qtr2,Qtr3,Qtr4)
          label='Maximum' format=dollar5.
   from orion.employee_donations
   where Paid_By="Cash or Check"
   order by 2 desc, Employee_ID;
quit;
```

SAS
enhancements

s103d03

13

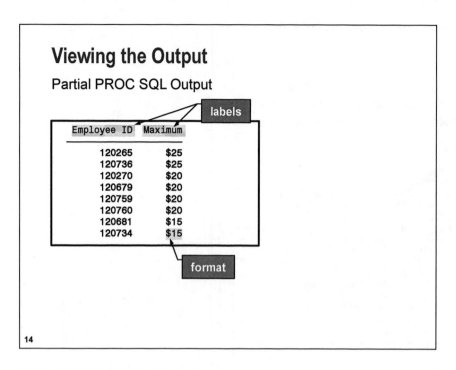

Viewing the Output

Partial PROC SQL Output

Adding Titles and Constant Text

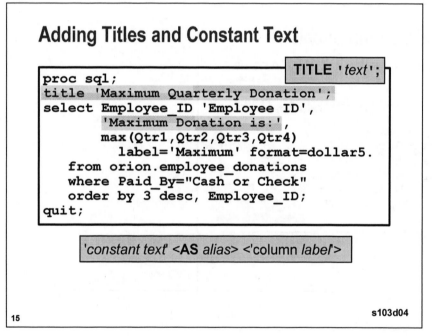

✏ TITLE and FOOTNOTE statements must precede the SELECT statement.

✏ When text is the only column specification, PROC SQL interprets it as a value, not a label.

Viewing the Output

Partial PROC SQL Output

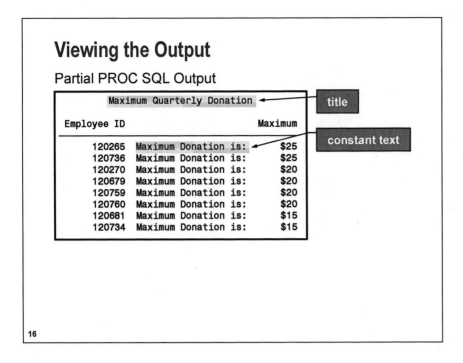

16

Adding a Row Number

PROC SQL <option(s)>;

```
proc sql number;
title 'Maximum Quarterly Donation';
select Employee_ID 'Employee ID',
       'Maximum Donation is:',
       max(Qtr1,Qtr2,Qtr3,Qtr4)
          label='Maximum' format=dollar5.
   from orion.employee_donations
   where Paid_By="Cash or Check"
   order by 3 desc, Employee_ID;
quit;
```

s103d05

17

🖉 There are some PROC SQL statement options that affect the SAS LISTING (Output) destination only: NOFLOW, FLOW=*n*, FLOW<=*n*, <*m*>> and DOUBLE. These options are ignored in other output destinations such as HTML.

Viewing the Output

Partial PROC SQL Output

```
              Maximum Quarterly Donation

   Row | Employee ID                        Maximum

     1         120265  Maximum Donation is:     $25
     2         120736  Maximum Donation is:     $25
     3         120270  Maximum Donation is:     $20
     4         120679  Maximum Donation is:     $20
     5         120759  Maximum Donation is:     $20
     6         120760  Maximum Donation is:     $20
     7         120681  Maximum Donation is:     $15
     8         120734  Maximum Donation is:     $15
```

18

PROC SQL Options

Options in the PROC SQL statement, such as line
numbers, remain in effect until they are changed, deleted,
or until a new PROC SQL statement is executed. Options
can be added, removed, or changed between PROC SQL
statements with the RESET statement.

```
PROC SQL option(s);
SELECT ...;

RESET option(s);

SELECT ...;
QUIT;
```

19

3.02 Quiz

Open the program file **s103a01**.

Submit the program and view the results.

Modify the program as follows:

- Add an option in the PROC SQL statement so that the rows of the first report are numbered.
- Add a new statement with the appropriate option after the first SELECT statement so that the rows of the second report are not numbered.

Resubmit the program and view the results.

Which option, NUMBER or NONUMBER, applies to the third report?

20   s103a01

Exercises

If you restarted your SAS session since the last exercise, open and submit the **libname.sas** program found in the data folder.

Level 1

1. **Enhancing Output by Ordering the Rows and Adding Titles and Formats**

   Open program **s103e01** and modify the query.

   a. Select only the **Employee_ID**, **Salary**, and **Tax** columns.

   b. Display the **Tax** and **Salary** columns using the COMMA10.2 format.

   c. Add labels to match the output below.

   d. Order the report by **Salary** in descending order.

   e. Add this title to the report: **Single Male Employee Salaries**.

Partial PROC SQL Output

```
                    Single Male Employee Salaries

                                          Federal
                                 Annual       Tax
                Employee ID      Salary  Withdrawn
                ----------------------------------
                     121141  194,885.00  64,961.67
                     120101  163,040.00  54,346.67
```

```
                                 120268   76,105.00   25,368.33
                                 120724   63,705.00   21,235.00
                                 120660   61,125.00   20,375.00

                                 ...
                                 121011   25,735.00    8,578.33
                                 121044   25,660.00    8,553.33
                                 121010   25,195.00    8,398.33
```

Level 2

2. Using Formats to Limit the Width of Columns in the Output

Write a query that retrieves the **Supplier_Name**, **Product_Group**, and **Product_Name** columns from the table **orion.product_dim**.

a. Add this title to the report: **Australian Clothing Products**.

b. Include only rows where the following are true: `Product_Category="Clothes"` and `Supplier_Country="AU"` (Australia).

c. To enable the report to print in portrait orientation, use formats to limit the width of the **Supplier_Name** column to 18 characters, **Group** to 12, and **Product_Name** to 30.

d. Label the columns **Supplier**, **Group**, and **Product**, respectively.

e. Order the report by **Product_Name**.

PROC SQL Output

```
                    Australian Clothing Products

   Supplier              Group                Product
   ───────────────────────────────────────────────────────────
   Typhoon Clothing      Street Wear          Tyfoon Flex Shorts
   Typhoon Clothing      Street Wear          Tyfoon Ketch T-Shirt
   Typhoon Clothing      Street Wear          Tyfoon Oliver Sweatshirt
```

Challenge

3. Enhancing Output with Multiple Techniques

Create a report that displays **Customer_ID** and the customer's name displayed as **LastName**, **FirstName**, and **Gender**, as well as the customer's age as of 02FEB2013. Use the data contained in the **orion.customer** table. Include only U.S. customers who were more than 50 years old on 02FEB2013. Present the data ordered by descending age and customer name. Give the report an appropriate title. Limit the space used to display the customer's name to a maximum of 20 characters so that the report can be printed in portrait orientation. The **Customer_ID** values must be displayed with leading zeros as shown in this sample report.

PROC SQL Output

```
                US Customers >50 Years Old as of 02FEB013

        Customer  Last Name,
              ID  First Name            Gender       Age
        ───────────────────────────────────────────────────
         0000056  Siferd, Roy              M          75
```

0000089	Lewis, Wynella	F	74
0000092	Celii, Lendon	M	64
0000023	Devereaux, Tulio	M	59
0000018	Asmussen, Tonie	M	55
0000017	Evans, Jimmie	M	54

3.2 Summarizing Data

Objectives

- Use functions to create summary queries.
- Group data and produce summary statistics for each group.
- Subset a query on summarized values.

25

Business Scenario

Management requested a report containing the total annual donations for each employee.

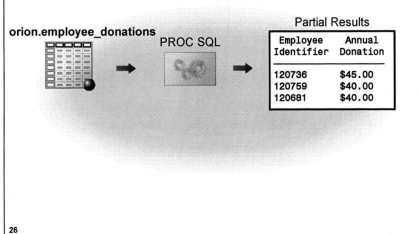

orion.employee_donations

PROC SQL

Partial Results

Employee Identifier	Annual Donation
120736	$45.00
120759	$40.00
120681	$40.00

26

Summary Functions: Across a Row

For a summary function with multiple arguments, nonmissing values are totaled across a row.

```
sum(Qtr1,Qtr2,Qtr3,Qtr4)
```

Partial **orion.employee_donations**

SAS Data Set

Employee_ID	Qtr1	Qtr2	Qtr3	Qtr4
120736	25	.	.	20
120759	15	20	5	.
120681	10	10	5	15
120679	.	20	5	15
120777	5	15	5	15

27

Summary Functions: Across a Row

Total each employee's annual cash donations.

```
proc sql;
select Employee_ID              SUM(col1, ..., coln)
       label='Employee Identifier',
       Qtr1,Qtr2,Qtr3,Qtr4,
       sum(Qtr1,Qtr2,Qtr3,Qtr4)
       label='Annual Donation'
       format=dollar5.
   from orion.employee_donations
   where Paid_By="Cash or Check"
   order by 6 desc;
quit;
```

28   s103d06

Viewing the Output

Partial PROC SQL Output

Employee Identifier	Qtr1	Qtr2	Qtr3	Qtr4	Annual Donation
120736	25	.	.	20	$45
120759	15	20	5	.	$40
120681	10	10	5	15	$40
120679	.	20	5	15	$40
120777	5	15	5	15	$40

29

3.03 Quiz

The following SELECT statements return the same results.

```
select sum(Qtr1,Qtr2,Qtr3,Qtr4)
   from orion.employee_donations;
```

```
select Qtr1+Qtr2+Qtr3+Qtr4
   from orion.employee_donations;
```

a. True
b. False

SAS Data Set

Employee_ID	Qtr1	Qtr2	Qtr3	Qtr4
120736	25	.	.	20
120759	15	20	5	.

30

Business Scenario

Management requested a report containing the total contributions for all employees in the first quarter.

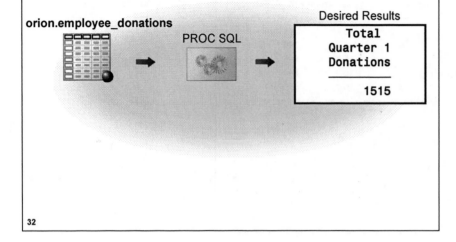

orion.employee_donations

PROC SQL

Desired Results

```
     Total
  Quarter 1
  Donations
-----------
        1515
```

32

Summary Functions: Down a Column

For a summary function with a single argument, nonmissing values are totaled down a column.

```
sum(Qtr1)
```

Partial **orion.employee_donations**

SAS Data Set

Employee_ID	Qtr1	Qtr2	Qtr3	Qtr4
120736	25	.	.	20
120759	15	20	5	.
120681	10	10	5	15
120679	.	20	5	15
120777	5	15	5	15

33

Summary Functions: Down a Column

Calculate the total of all charitable donations in quarter 1.

```
proc sql;                     SUM(argument)
select sum(Qtr1)
        'Total Quarter 1 Donations'
   from orion.employee_donations;
quit;
```

PROC SQL Output

```
      Total
    Quarter 1
    Donations
    _____

       1515
```

s103d07

34

Alternative Method: MEANS Procedure

Calculate the total all charitable donations in quarter 1.

```
proc means data=orion.employee_donations
           sum maxdec=0;
   var Qtr1;
run;
```

PROC MEANS Output

```
        Analysis Variable : Qtr1

                       Sum
              _____

                      1515
              _____
```

s103d07

35

Summary Functions: Recap

How a summary function works in SQL depends on the number of columns specified in the argument list.

- If the summary function specifies more than one column, the statistic is calculated for the row (using values from the listed columns).

```
sum(Qtr1,Qtr2,Qtr3,Qtr4)
```

- If the summary function specifies only one column, the statistic is calculated for the column (using values from one or more rows).

```
sum(Qtr1)
```

36

Commonly Used Summary Functions

Both ANSI SQL and SAS functions can be used in PROC SQL.

SQL	SAS	Description
AVG	MEAN	Returns the mean (average) value.
COUNT	FREQ, N	Returns the number of nonmissing values.
MAX	MAX	Returns the largest value.
MIN	MIN	Returns the smallest nonmissing value.
SUM	SUM	Returns the sum of nonmissing values.
	NMISS	Counts the number of missing values.
	STD	Returns the standard deviation.
	VAR	Returns the variance.

37

Business Scenario

Create a report that shows the total number of current Orion Star employees.

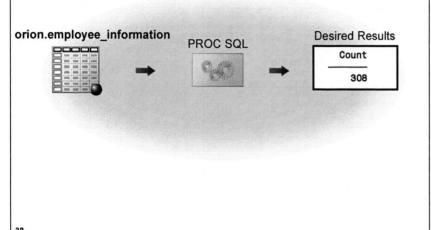

orion.employee_information

PROC SQL

Desired Results

Count
308

38

Summary Functions: COUNT Function

The *COUNT function* counts the number of rows returned by a query.

COUNT(*argument*)

```
proc sql;
select count(*) as Count
   from orion.employee_information
   where Employee_Term_Date is missing;
quit;
```

Argument value	Counts
* (asterisk)	All rows in a table or group
A column name	The number of nonmissing values in that column

39

s103d08

Viewing the Output

The COUNT function counts the number of rows returned by a query.

```
proc sql;
select count(Employee_ID) as Count
    from orion.employee_information
    where Employee_Term_Date is missing;
quit;
```

PROC SQL Output

Count
308

s103d08

40

3.04 Quiz

Open the program file **s103a02**. Submit the program and view the output.

1. How many rows did the first query create?
2. How many rows did the second query create?
3. In the second query's results, was the value in the **Average** column different for every gender listed?

s103a02

42

Remerging Summary Statistics

When a SELECT clause contains a column created by a summary function and a column that is **not** summarized, the summarized data is automatically appended to each row of the original data table (or *remerged*).

Employee_ Gender	Average
M	40476.92
M	40476.92
F	40476.92

Partial SAS Log

```
NOTE: The query requires remerging summary statistics back
      with the original data.
```

46

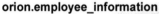

Most Database Management Systems do not enable remerging summary statistics. They generate an error instead.

Business Scenario

Calculate each male employee's salary as a percentage of all male employees' salaries.

orion.employee_information

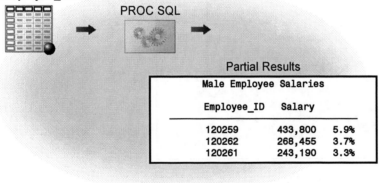

PROC SQL

Partial Results

Male Employee Salaries		
Employee_ID	Salary	
120259	433,800	5.9%
120262	268,455	3.7%
120261	243,190	3.3%

47

Using Remerged Summary Statistics

Calculate each male employee's salary as a percentage of all male employees' salaries. Display **Employee_ID**, **Salary**, and percentage in decreasing order of percentage.

```
proc sql;
title "Male Employee Salaries";
select Employee_ID, Salary format=comma12.,
       Salary / sum(Salary)
       'PCT of Total' format=percent6.2
   from orion.employee_information
   where Employee_Gender="M"
         and Employee_Term_Date is missing
   order by 3 desc;
quit;
title;
```

Select only the group of rows that you want to analyze.

48   ...

Using Remerged Summary Statistics

Calculate each male employee's salary as a percentage of all male employees' salaries. Display **Employee_ID**, **Salary**, and percentage in decreasing order of percentage.

```
proc sql;
title "Male Employee Salaries";
select Employee_ID, Salary format=comma12.,
       Salary / sum(Salary)
       'PCT of Total' format=percent6.2
   from orion.employee_information
   where Employee_Gender="M"
         and Employee_Term_Date is missing
   order by 3 desc;
quit;
title;
```

individual salary value for each row

divided by a remerged summary value (sum of all salaries)

49   s103d09

Viewing the Output

Partial PROC SQL Output

```
                     Male Employee Salaries

                             Employee
                               Annual    PCT of
            Employee_ID        Salary    Total
            ─────────────────────────────────────
               120259         433,800     5.9%
               120262         268,455     3.7%
               120261         243,190     3.3%
               121141         194,885     2.7%
               120101         163,040     2.2%
```

Partial SAS Log

```
NOTE: The query requires remerging summary statistics back
      with the original data.
```

50

This is a good example of SQL simplifying code. The following traditional SAS code produces similar results:

```
proc means data=orion.employee_information(where=(Employee_Gender="M"
                                    and Employee_Term_Date is missing))
          sum noprint;
   output out=work.summary sum=TotalSalary;
   var salary;
run;
data report;
   merge orion.employee_information (where=(Employee_Gender="M"
                               and Employee_Term_Date is missing))
         work.summary(keep=TotalSalary);
     retain Total 0;
     if _n_=1 then Total=TotalSalary;
     Percent=Salary / Total;
     keep Employee_ID Salary Percent;
     format salary comma12.2 Percent percent6.2;
run;
proc sort data=report;
   by descending Percent;
run;
title "Male Employee Salaries - Traditional SAS Programming";
proc print data=report noobs split='*';
        label Percent='*';
run;
title;
```

Remerging Summary Statistics

To change the default behavior, use either of the following:

- NOSQLREMERGE SAS system option
- PROC SQL NOREMERGE option

Resubmitting the query with the NOREMERGE option in effect produces no output and results in this SAS log error message:

```
ERROR: The query requires remerging summary statistics back with the
       original data. This is disallowed due to the NOREMERGE proc
       option or NOSQLREMERGE system option.
```

51   s103d09a

3.05 Quiz

Open the program file **s103a03**. Submit the query and review the output and the log. Answer the following questions:

1. How many rows of output are created?
2. What major difference is there in the log between this query's results and the second query in the previous activity?

52   s103a03

Business Scenario

Produce a report that determines the average salary by gender.

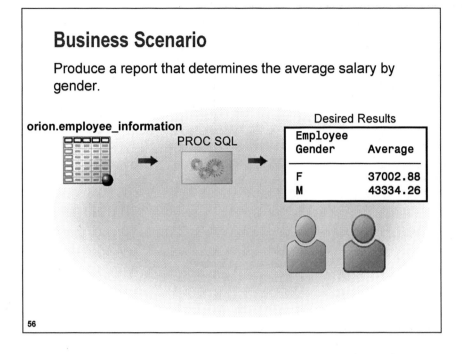

orion.employee_information

PROC SQL

Desired Results

Employee Gender	Average
F	37002.88
M	43334.26

56

Grouping Data

You can use the GROUP BY clause to do the following:

- classify the data into groups based on the values of one or more columns
- calculate statistics for each unique value of the grouping columns

```
proc sql;
title "Average Salary by Gender";
select Employee_Gender as Gender,
       avg(Salary) as Average
   from orion.employee_information
   where Employee_Term_Date is missing
   group by Employee_Gender;
quit;
```

GROUP BY *group-by-item<,..., group-by-item>*

57

s103d10

Viewing the Output

PROC SQL Output

```
            Average Salary by Gender

        Employee
        Gender              Average
        _____
        F                  37002.88
        M                  43334.26
```

58

3.06 Poll

Can you group by more than one column?

○ Yes

○ No

59

Business Scenario

Produce a report showing the count of employees in those departments that have at least 25 people. Display the results in descending order by count.

orion.employee_information

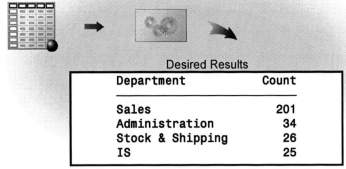

Desired Results

Department	Count
Sales	201
Administration	34
Stock & Shipping	26
IS	25

61

Step 1

Produce a report showing the number of employees in each department.

orion.employee_information

Partial Results

Department	Count
Accounts	17
Accounts Management	9
Administration	34

62

Analyzing Groups of Data

```
proc sql;
select Department, count(*) as Count
   from orion.employee_information
   group by Department;
quit;
```

63   s103d11

Step 2

Control the result to include only the departments that have
at least 25 people, with the departments in decreasing order.

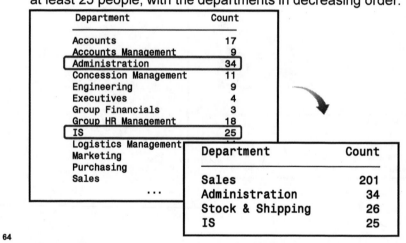

Department	Count
Accounts	17
Accounts Management	9
Administration	34
Concession Management	11
Engineering	9
Executives	4
Group Financials	3
Group HR Management	18
IS	25
Logistics Management	
Marketing	
Purchasing	
Sales	
...	

Department	Count
Sales	201
Administration	34
Stock & Shipping	26
IS	25

64

Selecting Groups with the HAVING Clause

The *HAVING clause* subsets groups based on the expression value.

```
proc sql;
select Department, count(*) as Count
   from orion.employee_information
   group by Department
   having Count ge 25
   order by Count desc;
quit;
```

> **GROUP BY** *group-by-item <,...,group-by-item>*
> **HAVING** *sql-expression*

65

s103d12

Viewing the Output

PROC SQL Output

Department	Count
Sales	201
Administration	34
Stock & Shipping	26
IS	25

66

WHERE Clause versus HAVING Clause

- The WHERE clause is evaluated **before** a row is available for processing and determines which individual rows are available for grouping.

> **WHERE** *sql-expression*

- The HAVING clause is processed **after** the GROUP BY clause and determines which groups are displayed.

> **HAVING** *sql-expression*

67

3.07 Quiz

Which syntax will select **Job_Title** values with a total **Bonus** value greater than $10,000?

1.
```
select Job_Title, sum(Salary*0.1) as Bonus
     from orion.employee_information
     group by Job_Title
     having Bonus > 10000;
```

2.
```
select Job_Title, sum(Salary*0.1) as Bonus
     from orion.employee_information
     where Bonus > 10000
     group by Job_Title;
```

3. both of the above
4. neither of the above

68

Business Scenario

Create a report that lists the following for each department:

- total number of managers
- total number of non-manager employees
- manager-to-employee (M/E) ratio

Below is a rough sketch of the desired report.

Department	Managers	Employees	M/E Ratio
Accounts	1	5	20%
Administration	2	20	10%

70

Business Data

Determine if an employee is a manager or a non-manager. The **Job_Title** column contains the information about each employee.

Department	Job_Title
Administration	Administration Manager
Administration	Secretary I
Administration	Office Assistant II

71

Counting Rows That Meet a Specified Criterion

How do you determine the rows that **do** have *Manager* in **Job_Title**, as well as rows that **do not**? You cannot use a WHERE clause to exclude either group.

```
Department           Job_Title

Administration       Administration Manager
Administration       Secretary I
Administration       Office Assistant II
```

Use the FIND function in a Boolean expression to identify rows that contain *Manager* in the **Job_Title** column.

72

FIND Function

The *FIND function* returns the starting position of the first occurrence of a substring within a string (character value). Find the starting position of the substring *Manager* in the character variable **Job_Title**.

```
find(Job_Title,"manager","i")
```

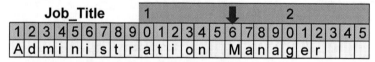

The value returned by the FIND function is 16.

FIND(*string, substring<,modifier(s)><,startpos>*)

73

string	constant, variable, or expression to be searched
substring	constant, variable, or expression sought within the string
modifiers	I=ignore case, T=trim trailing blanks
startpos	an integer specifying the start position and direction of the search

Using Boolean Expressions

Part 1: Use a Boolean expression to determine if an employee is a manager.

```
proc sql;
select Department, Job_Title,
       (find(Job_Title,"manager","i")>0)
       "Manager"
   from orion.employee_information;
quit;
```

✎ Boolean expressions evaluate to true (1) or false (0).

- If **Job_Title** contains *Manager*, the value is 1.
- If **Job_Title** does not contain *Manager*, the value is 0.

s103d13

74

Viewing the Output

Partial PROC SQL Output

Department	Job_Title	Manager
Administration	Administration Manager	1 ⬅
Administration	Secretary I	0
Administration	Office Assistant II	0
Administration	Office Assistant III	0
Administration	Warehouse Assistant II	0
Administration	Warehouse Assistant I	0
Administration	Warehouse Assistant III	0
Administration	Security Guard II	0
Administration	Security Guard I	0
Administration	Security Guard II	0
Administration	Security Manager	1 ⬅

75

Using Boolean Expressions

Part 2: Calculate the statistics requested.

```
proc sql;
title "Manager-to-Employee Ratios";
select Department,
       sum((find(Job_Title,"manager","i")>0))
          as Managers,
       sum((find(Job_Title,"manager","i")=0))
          as Employees,
       calculated Managers/calculated Employees
          "M/E Ratio" format=percent8.1
   from orion.employee_information
   group by Department;
quit;
```

76   s103d14

Viewing the Output

PROC SQL Output

```
                     Manager-to-Employee Ratios

                                                          M/E
   Department                   Managers   Employees     Ratio

   Accounts                         3          14        21.4%
   Accounts Management              1           8        12.5%
   Administration                   5          29        17.2%
   Concession Management            1          10        10.0%
   Engineering                      1           8        12.5%
   Executives                       0           4         0.0%
   Group Financials                 0           3         0.0%
   Group HR Management              3          15        20.0%
   IS                               2          23         8.7%
   Logistics Management             6           8        75.0%
   Marketing                        6          14        42.9%
   Purchasing                       3          15        20.0%
   Sales                            0         201         0.0%
   Sales Management                 5           6        83.3%
   Secretary of the Board           0           2         0.0%
   Stock & Shipping                 5          21        23.8%
   Strategy                         0           2         0.0%
```

77

 ## Exercises

If you restarted your SAS session since the last exercise, open and submit the **libname.sas** program found in the data folder.

Level 1

4. Summarizing Data

Create a report that displays the number of employees residing in each city.

a. Use the **orion.employee_addresses** table.

b. Use the **City** column and the COUNT(*) function.

c. Group the data and order the output by **City**.

d. Add this title to the report: **Cities Where Employees Live**.

PROC SQL Output

Cities Where Employees Live	
City	Count
Melbourne	41
Miami-Dade	109
Philadelphia	95
San Diego	112
Sydney	67

5. Using SAS Functions

Create a report that includes each employee's age at time of employment.

a. The report should contain the columns **Employee_ID**, **Birth_Date**, **Employee_Hire_Date**, and **Age**.

b. Obtain the data for the report from the **orion.employee_payroll** table.

c. Calculate **Age** as `int((Employee_Hire_Date-Birth_Date)/365.25)`.

d. Add this title to the report: **Age at Employment**.

e. Display **Birth_Date** and **Employee_Hire_Date** values using the MMDDYY10. format.

f. Label each column as shown in the following sample report:

Partial PROC SQL Output

Age at Employment			
Employee ID	Birth Date	Hire Date	Age
120101	08/18/1980	07/01/2007	26
120102	08/11/1973	06/01/1993	19
120103	01/22/1953	01/01/1978	24
120104	05/11/1958	01/01/1985	26
120105	12/21/1978	05/01/2003	24
120106	12/23/1948	01/01/1978	29
120107	01/21/1953	02/01/1978	25

Level 2

6. Summarizing Data

   a. Using data contained in the **orion.customer** table, create a report that shows the following statistics for each country:

      1) total number of customers

      2) total number of male customers

      3) total number of female customers

      4) percent of all customers that are male (**Percent Male**)

   b. Add this title to the report: **Customer Demographics: Gender by Country**.

   c. Arrange the report by value of **Percent Male** so that the country with the lowest value is listed first, with the remaining countries following in ascending order.

```
            Customer Demographics: Gender by Country

      Customer                                     Percent
      Country    Customers       Men     Women       Male
      _____

      ZA                 4         1         3        25%
      CA                15         7         8        47%
      US                28        15        13        54%
      AU                 8         5         3        63%
      DE                10         7         3        70%
      IL                 5         5         0       100%
      TR                 7         7         0       100%
```

   Hint: The Boolean expression (**Gender="M"**) evaluates as 1 when the value of **Gender** is *M* and 0 when the value of **Gender** is *F*.

7. Summarizing Data in Groups

Use the **orion.customer** table to determine the number of Orion Star customers of each gender in each country. Display columns named **Country**, **Male Customers**, and **Female Customers**. Display only those countries that have more female customers than male customers. Order the report by descending female customers. Add this title to the report: **Countries with More Female than Male Customers**.

PROC SQL Output

```
        Countries with More Female than Male Customers

                      Male       Female
            Country  Customers  Customers
            _____

            CA           7          8
            ZA           1          3
```

Challenge

8. Advanced Summarizing Data in Groups

Use the **orion.employee_addresses** table to create a report that displays the countries and cities where Orion Star employees reside, and the number of employees in each city. Include only one row per country/city combination. Display the values in country/city order, and give the report an appropriate title.

PROC SQL Output

```
                    Countries and Cities Where Employees Live

            Country  City                          Employees
                                                 _____

            AU       Melbourne                           41
            AU       Sydney                              67
            US       Miami-Dade                         109
            US       Philadelphia                        95
            US       San Diego                          112
```

Hint: Some data might not have consistent capitalization.

3.3 Solutions

Solutions to Exercises

1. Enhancing Output by Ordering the Rows and Adding Titles and Formats

```
*** s103s01 ***;
proc sql;
title "Single Male Employee Salaries";
select Employee_ID 'Employee ID',
       Salary format=comma10.2 'Annual Salary',
       Salary/3 format=comma10.2 as Tax
         'Federal Tax Withdrawn'
   from orion.employee_payroll
   where Marital_Status="S"
         and Employee_Gender ="M"
         and Employee_Term_Date is missing
   order by Salary desc;
quit;
title;
```

2. Using Formats to Limit the Width of Columns in the Output

```
*** s103s02 ***;
proc sql;
title "Australian Clothing Products";
select Supplier_Name 'Supplier'format=$18.,
       Product_Group 'Group' format=$12.,
       Product_Name 'Product' format=$30.
   from orion.product_dim
   where Supplier_Country="AU"
```

```
            and Product_Category="Clothes"
      order by Product_Name;
quit;
title;
```

3. Enhancing Output with Multiple Techniques

```
*** s103s03 ***;
proc sql;
title "US Customers >50 Years Old as of 02FEB2013";
select Customer_ID format=z7. 'Customer ID',
       catx(', ',Customer_LastName,Customer_FirstName)
       format=$20. 'Last Name, First Name' as Name,
       Gender 'Gender',
       int(('02feb2013'd-Birth_Date)/365.25) as Age
   from orion.customer
   where Country="US"
         and calculated Age>50
   order by Age desc, Name;
quit;
title;
```

4. Summarizing Data

```
*** s103s04 ***;

proc sql;
title "Cities Where Employees Live";
select City, Count(*) as Count
   from orion.employee_addresses
   group by City
   order by City;
quit;
title;
```

5. Using SAS Functions

```
*** s103s05 ***;

proc sql;
title "Age at Employment";
select Employee_ID 'Employee ID',
       Birth_Date format=mmddyy10. 'Birth Date',
       Employee_Hire_Date format=mmddyy10. 'Hire Date',
       int((Employee_Hire_Date-Birth_Date)/365.25)as Age 'Age'
   from orion.employee_payroll;
quit;
title;
```

6. Summarizing Data

```
*** s103s06 ***;

proc sql;
title "Customer Demographics: Gender by Country";
```

```
select Country, Count(*) as Customers,
       sum(Gender="M") as Men,
       sum(Gender ="F") as Women,
       calculated Men/calculated Customers 'Percent Male'
          format=percent6.1
   from orion.customer
   group by Country
   order by 5;
quit;
title;
```

7. Summarizing Data in Groups

```
*** s103s07 ***;

proc sql;
title "Countries with more Female than Male Customers";
select Country 'Country',
       sum(Gender="M") as M "Male Customers",
       sum(Gender="F") as F "Female Customers"
   from orion.customer
   group by Country
   having F > M
   order by F desc;
quit;
title;
```

8. Advanced Summarizing Data in Groups

```
*** s103s08 ***;

proc sql;
title "Countries and Cities Where Employees Live";
select upcase(Country) 'Country',
       propcase(City) 'City',
       count(*) 'Employees'
   from orion.employee_addresses
   group by 1,2
   order by 1,2;
quit;
title;
```

Items of interest:

- **Country** and **City** columns – The case of the data values is inconsistent. Sorting by column position uses the data in the intermediate results set, which was already corrected for case using SAS functions.

- Sorting by column name, even if you use column aliases (as **Country**, as **City**), produces duplicates in the output, although the data displayed appears to be identical. This happens because, by default, the ORDER BY and GROUP BY clauses operate on the **Country** and **City** data values found in the original table, before case correction. To ensure that you get the desired results, specify column position numbers in the GROUP BY and ORDER BY clauses instead of column names. This causes SQL to group by and sort by the values in the intermediate result set (corrected data) instead of the values in the original table.

Code demonstrating *incorrect* results:

```
*** s103s08 ***;
proc sql;
title "Countries and Cities Where Employees Live";
title2 "Incorrect Solution: Improper grouping due to Case issues";
title3 "Even with DISTINCT specified, duplicates remain";
select upcase(Country),
       propcase(City),
       count(*) 'Employees'
   from orion.employee_addresses
   group by country, city
   order by country, city;
quit;
title;
```

Solutions to Student Activities (Polls/Quizzes)

3.01 Multiple Choice Poll – Correct Answer

Which ORDER BY clause orders a report by descending **State** and descending **City**?

a. `order by desc State, City`

b. `order by State, City desc`

c. `order by State desc, City desc`

d. `order by desc State, desc City`

9

3.02 Quiz – Correct Answer

Open the program file **s103a01**.

Submit the program and view the results.

Modify the program as follows:

- Add an option in the PROC SQL statement so that the rows of the first report are numbered.
- Add a new statement with the appropriate option after the first SELECT statement so that the rows of the second report are not numbered.

Resubmit the program and view the results.

Which option, NUMBER or NONUMBER, applies to the third report?

The NONUMBER option applies to the third report.

21

3.03 Quiz – Correct Answer

The following SELECT statements return the same results.

```
select sum(Qtr1,Qtr2,Qtr3,Qtr4)
   from orion.employee_donations;
```

```
select Qtr1+Qtr2+Qtr3+Qtr4
   from orion.employee_donations;
```

a. True
b. False

The addition operator returns a missing value if any operand is missing.

31

3.04 Quiz – Correct Answer

1. How many rows did the first query create?

```
proc sql;
select 'The Average Salary is:',
       avg(Salary)
   from orion.employee_information
   where Employee_Term_Date is missing;
quit;
```

One row

```
  _____

  The Average Salary is:   40476.92
```

43   s103a02

3.04 Quiz – Correct Answer

2. How many rows did the second query create?

```
proc sql;
select Employee_Gender,
       avg(Salary) as Average
   from orion.employee_information
   where Employee_Term_Date is missing;
quit;
```

The output contains 308 rows. This is the number of rows returned by the COUNT(*) function in program s103d08.

44   s103a02

3.04 Quiz – Correct Answer

3. In the second query's results, was the value in the average column different for every gender listed? **no**

Every row contained the same Average value, which is the overall average salary for the entire table.

Employee_ Gender	Average
M	40476.92
M	40476.92
M	40476.92
F	40476.92
F	40476.92

s103a02

45

3.05 Quiz – Correct Answer

1. How many rows of output are created?

```
proc sql number;
select Employee_Gender,
       avg(Salary) as Average
   from orion.employee_information
   where Employee_Term_Date is missing
   group by Employee_Gender;
quit;
```

two rows

Row	Employee_ Gender	Average
1	F	37002.88
2	M	43334.26

53

3.05 Quiz – Correct Answer

2. What major difference is there in the log between this query's results and the second query in the previous activity?

SAS log notes from the previous activity:

```
NOTE: The query requires remerging summary statistics back
with the original data.
NOTE: PROCEDURE SQL used (Total process time):
      real time            0.01 seconds
      cpu time             0.01 seconds
```

SAS log notes from this activity:

```
NOTE: PROCEDURE SQL used (Total process time):
      real time            0.01 seconds
      cpu time             0.01 seconds
```

There was no note about remerging statistics.

54

3.06 Poll – Correct Answer

Can you group by more than one column?
◉ Yes
○ No

60

3.07 Quiz – Correct Answer

Which syntax will select **Job_Title** values with a total **Bonus** value greater than $10,000?

1.
```
select Job_Title, sum(Salary*0.1) as Bonus
    from orion.employee_information
    group by Job_Title
    having Bonus > 10000;
```

2.
```
select Job_Title, sum(Salary*0.1) as Bonus
    from orion.employee_information
    where Bonus > 10000
    group by Job_Title;
```

3. both of the above
4. neither of the above

69

Chapter 4   SQL Joins

4.1 Introduction to SQL Joins

Objectives

- Identify different ways to combine data horizontally from multiple tables.
- Distinguish between inner and outer SQL joins.
- Understand the Cartesian product.

3

Business Scenario

Management has requested multiple reports. You have to understand how to combine the data from the tables to complete these requests.

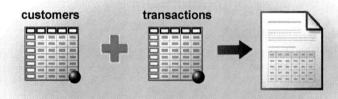

4

Exploring the Data

customers

ID	Name
101	Smith
104	Jones
102	Blank

transactions

ID	Action	Amount
102	Purchase	$100
103	Return	$52
105	Return	$212

The **customers** table is representative of a customer dimension table. There would be additional columns with data about our customers including address, age, and so on.

The **transactions** table is representative of a fact table. There would be columns holding all the key column data, **Product_ID**, **Employee_ID**, and so on.

5

Combining Data from Multiple Tables

SQL uses *joins* to combine tables horizontally. Requesting a join involves matching data from one row in one table with a corresponding row in a second table. Matching is typically performed on one or more columns in the two tables.

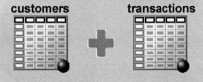

6

4.01 Multiple Choice Poll

Which of these DATA step statements is used to combine tables horizontally?

a. SET
b. APPEND
c. MERGE
d. INPUT
e. INFILE

7

Types of Joins

PROC SQL supports two types of joins:
Inner joins return only matching rows.

Outer joins return all matching rows, plus nonmatching rows from one or both tables.

Left   Full   Right

9

✎ *Cross joins*, *natural joins*, and *union joins* are special cases of the standard join types.

A *cross join* is a Cartesian product.

A *natural join* automatically selects columns with the same name and type to use in determining matching rows.

A *union join* is similar to combining two tables with the OUTER UNION set operator.

Cartesian Product

A query that lists multiple tables in the FROM clause
without a WHERE clause produces all possible
combinations of rows from all tables. This result is called
a *Cartesian product*.

```
proc sql;
select *
    from customers, transactions;
quit;
```

SELECT ...
FROM *table-name*, *table-name*
< , ...,*table-name* >;

To understand how SQL processes a join, it is helpful to
understand the concept of the Cartesian product.

10   s104d01

Building the Cartesian Product

customers

ID	Name
101	Smith
104	Jones
102	Blank

transactions

ID	Action	Amount
102	Purchase	$100
103	Return	$52
105	Return	$212

Result Set

ID	Name	ID	Action	Amount
101	Smith	102	Purchase	$100
101	Smith	103	Return	$52
101	Smith	105	Return	$212
104	Jones	102	Purchase	$100
104	Jones	103	Return	$52
104	Jones	105	Return	$212
102	Blank	102	Purchase	$100
102	Blank	103	Return	$52
102	Blank	105	Return	$212

19   ...

Building the Cartesian Product

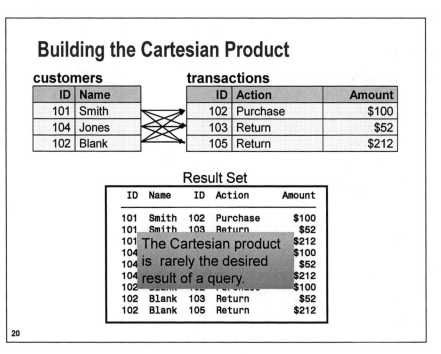

Non-Matching Data in the Cartesian Product

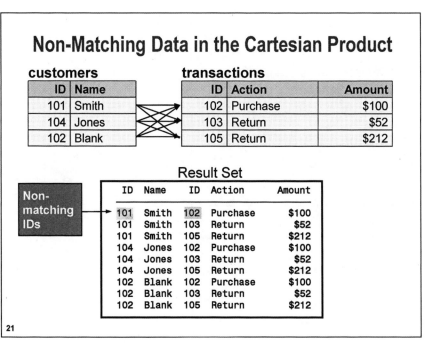

Size of the Cartesian Product

customers

ID	Name
101	Smith
104	Jones
102	Blank

transactions

ID	Action	Amount
102	Purchase	$100
103	Return	$52
105	Return	$212

Result Set

ID	Name	ID	Action	Amount
101	Smith	102	Purchase	$100
101	Smith	103	Return	$52
101	Smith	105	Return	$212
104	Jones	102	Purchase	$100
104	Jones	103	Return	$52
104	Jones	105	Return	$212
102	Blank	102	Purchase	$100
102	Blank	103	Return	$52
102	Blank	105	Return	$212

9 rows

22

Size of the Cartesian Product

The number of rows in a Cartesian product is the product of the number of rows in the contributing tables.

$$3 \times 3 = 9$$
$$1{,}000 \times 1{,}000 = 1{,}000{,}000$$
$$100{,}000 \times 100{,}000 = 10{,}000{,}000{,}000$$

Partial SAS Log

```
NOTE: The execution of this query involves performing one or more
      Cartesian product joins that cannot be optimized.
```

23

4.02 Quiz

How many rows and columns are returned from this query?

```
select *
   from customer2, transaction2;
```

customer2

ID	Name
101	Jones
101	Jones
102	Kent
102	Kent
104	Avery

transaction2

ID	Action	Amount
102	Purchase	$376
102	Return	$119
103	Purchase	$57
105	Purchase	$98

24   s104a01

4.2 Inner Joins

Objectives

- Join two or more tables on matching columns.
- Qualify column names to identify specific columns.
- Use a table alias to simplify the SQL code.
- Join two tables with alternative join syntax.

28

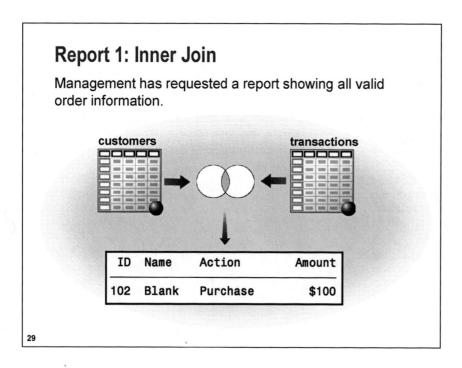

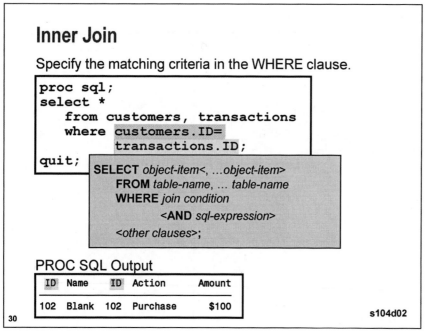

✎   The SQL Procedure Optimizer has algorithms from which it selects to optimize a join. For example, the optimizer might use a hashing algorithm when joining a small table with a large table.

A detailed paper on PROC SQL join optimization can be found here:
http://support.sas.com/techsup/technote/ts553.html

4.03 Quiz

Why are there two ID columns in the result?

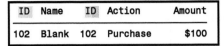

ID	Name	ID	Action	Amount
102	Blank	102	Purchase	$100

31

Qualifying the Column Names

When you specify columns with the same name from more than one table, it is necessary to qualify the column name.

```
proc sql;
select *
    from customers, transactions
    where customers.ID=
          transactions.ID;
quit;
```

table-name.column-name

s104d02

33

Setup for Quiz

Run program **s104a02** and review the results.

What message is displayed in the log when the program
is executed?

```
proc sql;
select *
   from customers, transactions
   where ID=ID;
quit;
```

34

4.04 Quiz

What message is displayed in the log when the program
is executed?

35

Completed Code for Report 1

To display the ID column only once in the results, qualify the ID column in the SELECT clause.

customers

ID	Name
101	Smith
104	Jones
102	Blank

transactions

ID	Action	Amount
102	Purchase	$100
103	Return	$52
105	Return	$212

```
select customers.ID, Name, Action, Amount
    from customers, transactions
    where customers.ID=transactions.ID;
```

ID	Name	Action	Amount
102	Blank	Purchase	$100

s104d03

37

Equijoins are inner joins where the join criteria specify equality for the identifying variables. Natural joins are equijoins in which SQL compares the values of all same-name columns in both tables and produces output containing **only one column** for results from same-name columns in the source tables. The rows in the tables are joined, based on matching values in same-name columns.

For example, the following natural join code would produce results identical to the query above:

```
proc sql;
select *
    from customers natural join transactions;
quit;
```

Abbreviating the Code

A *table alias* is a temporary, alternative name for a table. You can make the query easier to read by using table aliases.

SELECT *alias-1.object-item<, ...alias-2.object-item>*
    FROM *table-name <AS> alias-1,*
        table-name <AS> alias-2
    WHERE *join-condition(s)*
    <other clauses>;

The AS keyword is optional in the table alias syntax.

38

Abbreviating the Code with a Table Alias

```
proc sql;
select c.ID, Name, Action, Amount
    from customers as c, transactions as t
    where c.ID=t.ID;
quit;
```

PROC SQL Output

ID	Name	Action	Amount
102	Blank	Purchase	$100

39

s104d04

SQL Inner Join versus DATA Step Merge

A PROC SQL inner join and the DATA step match merge can return the same results.

```
proc sql;
select c.ID, Name, Action,
       Amount
  from customers as c,
       transactions as t
  where c.ID=t.ID;
quit;
```

```
data orders;
   merge customers(in=c)
         transactions(in=t);
   by ID;
   if c=1 and t=1;
run;
proc print data=orders;
run;
```

40

s104d04

SQL Inner Join versus DATA Step Merge

A PROC SQL inner join and the DATA step match merge will not always return the same results.

customer2

ID	Name
101	Jones
101	Jones
102	Kent
102	Kent
104	Avery

transaction2

ID	Action	Amount
102	Purchase	$376
102	Return	$119
103	Purchase	$57
105	Purchase	$98

```
select *
   from customer2 as c2, transaction2 as t2
   where c2.ID=t2.ID;
```

ID	Name	ID	Action	Amount
102	Kent	102	Purchase	$376
102	Kent	102	Purchase	$376
102	Kent	102	Return	$119
102	Kent	102	Return	$119

s104d05

41

Setup for the Poll

Run program **s104a03** and review the results to determine how many rows (observations) the DATA step MERGE statement produces in the output table.

customer2

ID	Name
101	Jones
101	Jones
102	Kent
102	Kent
104	Avery

transaction2

ID	Action	Amount
102	Purchase	$376
102	Return	$119
103	Purchase	$57
105	Purchase	$98

```
data work.new;
   merge customer2 in=(InCust)
         transaction2 in=(InTrans);
   by ID;
   if InCust=1 and InTrans=1;
run;

proc print data=work.new;
run;
```

s104a03

42

4.05 Multiple Choice Poll

How many rows (observations) result from the DATA step MERGE statement in program **s104a03**?

a. 2

b. 4

c. 6

d. 20

e. none of the above

43

Compare SQL Join and DATA Step Merge

Key Points	SQL Join	DATA Step Merge
Explicit sorting of data before join/merge	Not required	Required
Same-name columns in join/merge expressions	Not required	Required
Equality in join or merge expressions	Not required	Required

45

Alternative Join Syntax

This alternative syntax names the join type and includes an ON clause.

```
select c.ID, Name, Action, Amount
   from customers as c
        inner join
        transactions as t
        on c.ID=t.ID;
```

SELECT *object-item* <, ...*object-item*>
FROM *table-name* <<**AS**> *alias*>
INNER JOIN
table-name <<**AS**> *alias*>
ON *join-condition(s)*
WHERE *sql-expression*
<*other clauses*>;

46

s104d06

Up to 256 tables can be joined using the alternative join syntax. The join processes two tables at a time, until all tables have been joined.

```
select *
   from one inner join two
           on one.id=two.id
        inner join three
           on one.id=three.id
        inner join four
           on one.id=four.id;
```

4.06 Quiz

How many tables can be combined using the following PROC SQL syntax?

```
proc sql;
select *
   from table-name,..., table-name
   where sql-expression;
quit;
```

47

Exercises

If you restarted your SAS session since the last exercise, open and submit the **libname.sas** program found in the data folder.

Level 1

1. Inner Joins

Produce a report containing **Employee_Name** and calculated years of service (YOS) as of February 1, 2013, by joining **orion.employee_addresses** and **orion.employee_payroll** on **Employee_ID**. Label the columns and provide two title lines, as shown in the sample output. Limit the report to employees where YOS > 30. Order the output alphabetically by **Employee_Name**.

- The **orion.employee_addresses** table contains the **Employee_Name** column.

- The **orion.employee_payroll** table contains the **Employee_Hire_Date** column.

- Both **orion.employee_addresses** and **orion.employee_payroll** contain columns named **Employee_ID**.

- Use TITLE1 and TITLE2 statements to produce title lines as indicated in the sample report:

Partial PROC SQL Output

```
                     Employees With More Than 30 Years of Service
                              As of February 1, 2013


                                                      Years of
                    Name                               Service

                    Abbott, Ray                             33
                    Banchi, Steven                          35
                    Blackley, James                         35
                    Bleu, Henri Le                          35
                    Branly, Wanda                           35
                    Buddery, Jeannette                      35
                    Campbell, Carston                       35
                    Capps, Ramond                           35
```

 Age and years of service calculations can be difficult to render precisely. In this course, you use the following:

int(('1FEB2013'd - Employee_Hire_Date)/365.25) as YOS

For a more in-depth discussion, see "Accurately Calculating Age with Only One Line of Code" at **http://support.sas.com/kb/24/808.html**.

Level 2

2. Creating a Summary Report from Two Tables

The head of the Sales Department wants to know how many of each product was sold since the beginning of 2010. The report should include the product ID, the product name, and the total sold for that product and ordered to match the output shown below.

The data that you need can be found in the listed columns of the following tables:

- **orion.product_dim** contains
  - **Product_ID**
  - **Product_Name.**
- **orion.order_fact** contains
  - **Product_ID**
  - **Quantity.**

Partial PROC SQL Output

```
                Total Quantities Sold by Product ID and Name

                                                        Total
           Product ID  Product Name                      Sold
           ─────────────────────────────────────────────────
           230100600022  Expedition10,Medium,Right,Blue Ribbon      9
           240700100001  Armour L                                   8
           230100600016  Expedition Zero,Medium,Right,Charcoal      8
           230100700011  Hurricane 4                                8
           230100500056  Knife                                      8
           230100600030  Outback Sleeping Bag, Large,Left,Blue/Black  8
           240500100017  A-team Sweat Round Neck, Small Logo        7
           240700200010  Bat - Home Run S                           7
           220101400387  N.d.gear Cap                               7
```

Challenge

3. **Joining Multiple Tables**

   Create a report showing Orion Star catalog and Internet customers residing in the U.S. or Australia who purchased foreign-manufactured products (that is, a product that was not manufactured in their country of residence). The report should be titled **US and Australian Catalog and Internet Customers Purchasing Foreign Manufactured Products** and should display the customers' names and the number of foreign purchases made. Present the information so that those with the largest number of purchases appear at the top of the report, and customers who have the same number of purchases are displayed in alphabetical order.

   Employee_ID *99999999* is a dummy ID that can be used to identify catalog and Internet orders. The data that you need can be found in the listed columns of the following tables:

   - **orion.product_dim** contains
     - **Product_ID**
     - **Supplier_Country.**
   - **orion.order_fact** contains
     - **Product_ID**
     - **Employee_ID**
     - **Customer_ID.**
   - **orion.customer** contains
     - **Customer_ID**
     - **Country.**

Partial PROC SQL Output

```
                US and Australian Catalog and Internet Customers
                     Purchasing Foreign Manufactured Products

             Name                                    Purchases
             ─────────────────────────────────────────────────
             Candy Kinsey                                10
             Phenix Hill                                  7
             Cynthia Mccluney                             5
             Korolina Dokter                              5
             Najma Hicks                                  4
             Robert Bowerman                              4
```

4.3 Outer Joins

Objectives

- Join two tables on matching columns and include non-matching rows from one table.
- Join two tables on matching columns and include non-matching rows from both tables.
- Compare outer joins and DATA step merges.

52

Outer Joins

You can retrieve both non-matching and matching rows using an outer join.

Outer joins include left, full, and right outer joins. Many tables can be referenced in outer joins. The tables are processed two tables at a time.

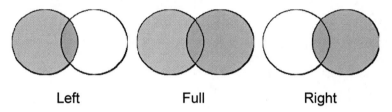

| Left | Full | Right |

53

Report 2: Outer Joins

You have been asked for a report that displays *all* customers and any recent transactions that they have completed.

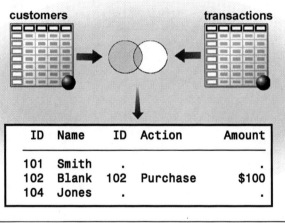

ID	Name	ID	Action	Amount
101	Smith	.		.
102	Blank	102	Purchase	$100
104	Jones	.		.

54

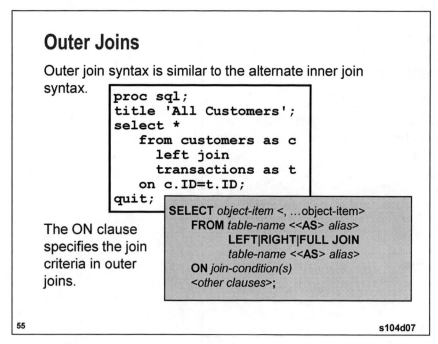

Outer Joins

Outer join syntax is similar to the alternate inner join syntax.

```
proc sql;
title 'All Customers';
select *
    from customers as c
       left join
       transactions as t
    on c.ID=t.ID;
quit;
```

The ON clause specifies the join criteria in outer joins.

SELECT *object-item* <, ...*object-item*>
   FROM *table-name* <<**AS**> *alias*>
       LEFT|RIGHT|FULL JOIN
       table-name <<**AS**> *alias*>
   ON *join-condition(s)*
   <*other clauses*>;

55   s104d07

The WHERE and ON clauses operate independently.

- The ON clause specifies the rows to be joined.

- The WHERE clause produces a subset of the results.

Viewing the Output

PROC SQL Output

	All Customers			
ID	Name	ID	Action	Amount
101	Smith	.		.
102	Blank	102	Purchase	$100
104	Jones	.		.

56

Determining Left and Right

Consider the position of the tables in the FROM clause.

- Left joins return all matching and non-matching rows from the *left* table and the matching rows from the *right* table.
- Right joins return all matching and non-matching rows from the *right* table and the matching rows from the *left* table.
- Full joins return all matching and non-matching rows from all of the tables.

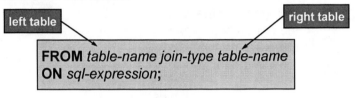

```
FROM table-name join-type table-name
ON sql-expression;
```

57

Left Join

customers

ID	Name
101	Smith
104	Jones
102	Blank

transactions

ID	Action	Amount
102	Purchase	$100
103	Return	$52
105	Return	$212

```
select *
   from customers c left join transactions t
   on c.ID = t.ID;
```

ID	Name	ID	Action	Amount
101	Smith	.		.
102	Blank	102	Purchase	$100
104	Jones	.		.

Includes all rows from the left table, even if there are no matching rows in the right table.

s104d08

58

Right Join

customers

ID	Name
101	Smith
104	Jones
102	Blank

transactions

ID	Action	Amount
102	Purchase	$100
103	Return	$52
105	Return	$212

```
select *
   from customers c right join transactions t
   on c.ID = t.ID;
```

ID	Name	ID	Action	Amount
102	Blank	102	Purchase	$100
.		103	Return	$52
.		105	Return	$212

Includes all rows from the right table, even if there are no matching rows in the left table.

59

s104d09

Full Join

customers

ID	Name
101	Smith
104	Jones
102	Blank

transactions

ID	Action	Amount
102	Purchase	$100
103	Return	$52
105	Return	$212

```
select *
   from customers c full join transactions t
   on c.ID = t.ID;
```

ID	Name	ID	Action	Amount
101	Smith	.		.
102	Blank	102	Purchase	$100
.		103	Return	$52
104	Jones	.		.
.		105	Return	$212

Includes all rows from both tables, even if there are no matching rows in either table

60

s104d10

4.07 Quiz

Given these two SELECT statements:

```
select *
   from customers left join transactions
   on customers.ID=transactions.ID;
```

```
select *
   from transactions right join customers
   on customers.ID=transactions.ID;
```

1. Will the result sets contain the same data?
2. What is the difference in the result sets?

s104d11

61

Report 3

Management is considering a matching spouse donation program. A report is needed showing employees who are married and make contributions to company-sponsored charities.

orion.employee_payroll   **orion.employee_donations**

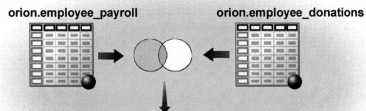

```
Employee_ID  Recipients
   121128    Cancer Cures, Inc.
   121131    Vox Victimas 40%, Conserve Nature, Inc. 60%
   121132    EarthSalvors 50%, Vox Victimas 50%
```

63

Business Data: Part 4

- The table **orion.employee_payroll** contains gender and marital status information.
- The table **orion.employee_donations** contains records only for those employees who donate to a charity via the company program.
- About half of all employees are married.

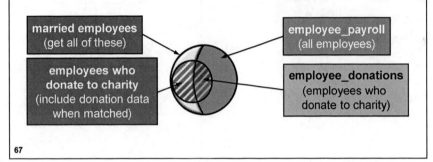

67

4.08 Multiple Choice Poll

For the report, you need the data for all married employees from **orion.employee_payroll**.
You also want to include the charity names from the **orion.employee_donations** table if **Employee_ID** matches. What type of join should you use to combine the information from these two tables?

 a. inner join
 b. left join
 c. full join
 d. none of the above

68

Completed Code for Report 3

This is the PROC SQL code that will generate the manager's requested report.

```
proc sql;
select p.Employee_ID, Recipients
   from orion.employee_payroll as p
        left join
        orion.employee_donations as d
   on p.Employee_ID=
      d.Employee_ID
   where Marital_Status="M";
quit;
```

✎ Output order is not guaranteed unless an ORDER
   BY clause is included.

70   s104d12

Viewing the Output

Partial PROC SQL Output (Rows 203–215)

```
Employee_ID  Recipients

    121128   Cancer Cures, Inc.
    121131   Vox Victimas 40%, Conserve Nature, Inc. 60%
    121132   EarthSalvors 50%, Vox Victimas 50%
    121133   Disaster Assist, Inc.
    121138   Cuidadores Ltd.
    121139
    121142   AquaMissions International 10%, Child Survivors 90%
    121143   Mitleid International 60%, Save the Baby Animals 40%
    121144
    121145   Save the Baby Animals
    121146
    121147   Cuidadores Ltd. 50%, Mitleid International 50%
    121148
```

71

DATA Step Merge

A DATA step with MERGE and BY statements combines tables similar to an SQL join. Columns are treated differently in the results.

customers

ID	Name
101	Smith
104	Jones
102	Blank

transactions

ID	Action	Amount
102	Purchase	$100
103	Return	$52
105	Return	$212

Customers must be sorted or indexed on column ID before a merge can be performed.

72

DATA Step Merge

A DATA step merge automatically overlays same-name columns.

```
data merged;
   merge customers transactions;
   by ID;
run;
proc print data=merged;
run;
```

```
ID     Name      Action      Amount

101    Smith                      .
102    Blank     Purchase      $100
103              Return         $52
104    Jones                      .
105              Return        $212
```

s104d13

73

SQL Join versus DATA Step Merge

SQL joins do not overlay same-name columns.

customers

ID	Name
101	Smith
104	Jones
102	Blank

transactions

ID	Action	Amount
102	Purchase	$100
103	Return	$52
105	Return	$212

```
proc sql;
select *
    from customers c full join transactions t
    on c.ID=t.ID;
quit;
```

ID	Name	ID	Action	Amount
101	Smith	.		.
102	Blank	102	Purchase	$100
.		103	Return	$52
104	Jones	.		.
.		105	Return	$212

74   s104d13

COALESCE Function

You can use the *COALESCE function* to overlay columns.
The COALESCE function returns the value of the first
nonmissing argument.

```
proc sql;
select coalesce(c.ID,t.ID) as ID,
        Name, Action, Amount
    from customers c full join transactions t
    on c.ID=t.ID;
quit;
```

COALESCE(*argument-1,argument-2<, ...argument-n>*)

75   s104d13

 The arguments in the COALESCE function can be a variable name, a constant, or an expression.
When all arguments are missing, COALESCE returns a missing value. All arguments must be of
the same type (character or numeric).

Viewing the Output

The COALESCE function returns a single ID column in the output.

ID	Name	Action	Amount
101	Smith		.
102	Blank	Purchase	$100
103		Return	$52
104	Jones		.
105		Return	$212

76

Comparing Inner Joins and Outer Joins

Key Points	Inner Join	Outer Join
Table Limit	256	256
Join Behavior	Returns matching rows only	Returns matching and nonmatching rows
Join Options	Matching rows only	LEFT, FULL, RIGHT
Syntax changes	▪ Multiple tables, separated by commas, in the FROM clause ▪ WHERE clause that specifies join criteria	ON clause that specifies join criteria

77

Tables can be joined on inequalities—for example:

```
proc sql;
title "List of things I could buy";
select Item_name, Price
   from budget, wish_list
   where budget.Cash_Available > wish_list.Price;
quit;
```

 **Exercises**

If you restarted your SAS session since the last exercise, open and submit the **libname.sas** program found in the data folder.

Level 1

4. **Outer Join**

   Join **orion.sales** and **orion.employee_addresses** on **Employee_ID** to create a report showing the names and cities of all Orion Star employees. If an employee is in the Sales Department, also show the job title. Present the report in alphabetical order by city, job title, and name.

   - The **orion.sales** table contains a record for every employee in the Sales Department and includes columns **Employee_ID** and **Job_Title**.

   - The **orion.employee_addresses** table contains a record for every employee and includes **Employee_ID**, **Employee_Name**, and **City**.

   Partial PROC SQL Output

Name	City	Job_Title
Blanton, Brig	Melbourne	
Catenacci, Reyne	Melbourne	
Dillin, Kerrin	Melbourne	
Fiocca, Jina	Melbourne	
Fouche, Madelaine	Melbourne	
Glattback, Ellis	Melbourne	
Graham-Rowe, Jannene	Melbourne	
Gromek, Gladys	Melbourne	
Harwood, Reece	Melbourne	
Hieds, Merle	Melbourne	
Horsey, Riu	Melbourne	
Mccleary, Bill	Melbourne	
Moffat, Trent	Melbourne	
Pettolino, Peter	Melbourne	
Povey, Liz	Melbourne	
Santomaggio, Pearl	Melbourne	
Sheedy, Sherie	Melbourne	
Streit, Russell	Melbourne	
Zhou, Tom	Melbourne	Sales Manager
Barcoe, Selina	Melbourne	Sales Rep. I
Chantharasy, Judy	Melbourne	Sales Rep. I
Duckett, Shani	Melbourne	Sales Rep. I
Osborn, Hernani	Melbourne	Sales Rep. I
Pa, Koavea	Melbourne	Sales Rep. I
Scordia, Randal	Melbourne	Sales Rep. I
Simms, Doungkamol	Melbourne	Sales Rep. I
Aisbitt, Sandy	Melbourne	Sales Rep. II
George, Vino	Melbourne	Sales Rep. II
Magrath, Brett	Melbourne	Sales Rep. II

Level 2

5.   Outer Join

Join the **orion.order_fact** and **orion.product_dim** tables to determine whether there are any items in the product dimension table that have never been sold.

4.4 Complex SQL Joins

Objectives

■ Perform a self-join (reflexive join).

81

Business Scenario

The chief sales officer wants to have a report with the name of all sales employees and the name of each employee's direct manager.

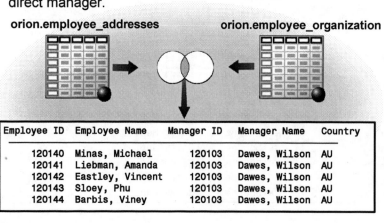

orion.employee_addresses   orion.employee_organization

Employee ID	Employee Name	Manager ID	Manager Name	Country
120140	Minas, Michael	120103	Dawes, Wilson	AU
120141	Liebman, Amanda	120103	Dawes, Wilson	AU
120142	Eastley, Vincent	120103	Dawes, Wilson	AU
120143	Sloey, Phu	120103	Dawes, Wilson	AU
120144	Barbis, Viney	120103	Dawes, Wilson	AU

82

Business Data

To return the employee name and the manager name, you need to read the **addresses** table twice.

1. Return the employee's ID and name.
2. Determine the ID of the employee's manager.
3. Return the manager's name.

addresses

EMP_ID	EMP_NAME
100	John
101	Sue

organization

EMP_ID	MGR_ID
100	101
101	57

EMP_ID	EMP_Name	MGR_ID	MGR_Name
100	John	101	Sue

85

Required Table Aliases

In order to read from the same table twice, it must be listed in the FROM clause twice. Here, a different table alias is required to distinguish the different uses.

```
from orion.employee_addresses as e,
     orion.employee_addresses as m,
```

FROM *table-name-1* <AS> *alias-1*,
table-name-1 <AS> *alias-2*

86

Required Table Aliases

```
select e.Employee_ID "Employee ID",
       e.Employee_Name "Employee Name",
       m.Employee_ID "Manager ID",
       m.Employee_Name "Manager Name",
       e.Country
  from orion.employee_addresses as e,
       orion.employee_addresses as m,
       orion.employee_organization as o
 where e.Employee_ID=o.Employee_ID and
       o.Manager_ID=m.Employee_ID and
       Department contains 'Sales'
 order by Country,4,1;
```

s104d14

87

Viewing the Output

Partial PROC SQL Output

Employee ID	Employee Name	Manager ID	Manager Name	Country
120140	Minas, Michael	120103	Dawes, Wilson	AU
120141	Liebman, Amanda	120103	Dawes, Wilson	AU
120142	Eastley, Vincent	120103	Dawes, Wilson	AU
120143	Sloey, Phu	120103	Dawes, Wilson	AU
120144	Barbis, Viney	120103	Dawes, Wilson	AU

88

Exercises

If you restarted your SAS session since the last exercise, open and submit the **libname.sas** program found in the data folder.

Level 1

6. Creating a Report with a Self-Join

Create a report of all trainees and temporary workers to include their ID, name, and job title and their manager's ID and name. Order the report by the employee's ID. Label the columns and title the report as shown in the sample output.

The data that you need can be found in the listed columns of the following tables:

- **orion.employee_addresses** contains
  - **Employee_ID**
  - **Employee_Name**.
- **orion.staff** contains
  - **Employee_ID**
  - **Job_Title**
  - **Manager_ID** (**Employee_ID** of the person's manager).

Partial PROC SQL Output

```
                         Trainee and Temporary Employees

Employee                                                  Manager
      ID   Employee_ Name        Employee Job Title            ID   Manager Name
--------------------------------------------------------------------------------
  120181   Cantatore, Lorian     Temp. Sales Rep.          120103   Dawes, Wilson
  120182   Barreto, Geok-Seng    Temp. Sales Rep.          120103   Dawes, Wilson
  120183   Blanton, Brig         Temp. Sales Rep.          120103   Dawes, Wilson
  120184   Moore, Ari            Temp. Sales Rep.          120103   Dawes, Wilson
  120185   Bahlman, Sharon       Temp. Sales Rep.          120103   Dawes, Wilson
  120186   Quinby, Merryn        Temp. Sales Rep.          120103   Dawes, Wilson
  120187   Catenacci, Reyne      Temp. Sales Rep.          120103   Dawes, Wilson
  120188   Baran, Shanmuganathan Temp. Sales Rep.          120103   Dawes, Wilson
  120189   Lachlan, Mihailo      Temp. Sales Rep.          120103   Dawes, Wilson
  120190   Czernezkyi, Ivor      Trainee                   120103   Dawes, Wilson
  120191   Graham-Rowe, Jannene  Trainee                   120103   Dawes, Wilson
```

Level 2

7. Joining Multiple Tables

Create a report of Orion Star employees with more than 30 years of service as of February 1, 2013. Display the employee's name, years of service, and the name of the employee's manager. Order the report alphabetically by manager name, by descending years of service, and then alphabetically by employee name. Label the columns and title the report as shown in the sample output.

The data that you need can be found in the listed columns of the following tables:

- **orion.employee_addresses** contains
  - **Employee_ID**
  - **Employee_Name**.
- **orion.employee_payroll** contains
  - **Employee_ID**

– **Employee_Hire_Date**.

- **orion.employee_organization** contains

  – **Employee_ID**

  – **Manager_ID** (**Employee_ID** of the person's manager).

Partial PROC SQL Output

```
                 Employees with More Than 30 Years of Service
                           As of February 1, 2013

                                           Years of
            Employee Name                  Service   Manager Name

            Marion, Chiorene                    35   Ardskin, Elizabeth
            Zied, Ahmed                         35   Ardskin, Elizabeth
            Droste, Victor                      31   Ardskin, Elizabeth
            Parker, U'Vonda                     31   Ardskin, Elizabeth
            Buddery, Jeannette                  35   Billington, Kareen
```

4.5 Solutions

Solutions to Exercises

1. **Inner Joins**

```
*** s104s01 ***;

proc sql;
title "Employees With More Than 30 Years of Service";
title2 "As of February 1, 2013";
select Employee_Name 'Name',
       int(('1FEB2013'd-Employee_Hire_Date)/365.25)
       as YOS 'Years of Service'
   from orion.employee_addresses as a,
        orion.employee_payroll as p
   where a.Employee_ID=p.Employee_ID
         and calculated YOS gt 30
   order by Employee_Name;
quit;
title;
```

2. **Creating a Summary Report from Two Tables**

```
*** s104s02 ***;

proc sql;
title 'Total Quantities Sold by Product ID and Name';
select p.Product_ID,
       Product_Name,
       sum(Quantity) 'Total Sold'
   from orion.product_dim as p,
        orion.order_fact as o
   where p.Product_ID = o.Product_ID
```

```
      group by p.Product_ID, Product_Name
      order by 3 desc, Product_Name;
quit;
title;
```

3. Joining Multiple Tables

```
*** s104s03 ***;

proc sql;
title  "US and Australian Catalog and Internet Customers";
title2 "Purchasing Foreign Manufactured Products";
select Customer_Name 'Name', Count(*) 'Purchases'
        as Count
   from orion.product_dim as p,
        orion.order_fact as o,
        orion.customer as c
   where p.Product_ID=o.Product_ID
        and o.Customer_ID=c.Customer_ID
        and Employee_ID=99999999
        and p.Supplier_Country ne Country
        and Country in ('US','AU')
   group by Customer_Name
   order by Count desc, Customer_Name;
quit;
title;
```

4. Outer Join

```
*** s104s04 ***;

proc sql;
select Employee_Name 'Name' format=$35.,
        City, Job_Title
   from orion.employee_addresses as a
        left join
        orion.sales as s
        on a.Employee_ID=s.Employee_ID
   order by City, Job_Title, Employee_Name;
quit;
```

5. Outer Join

```
*** s104s05 **;

proc sql;
title 'Products That Have Not Been Sold';
select Product_Name,
        p.Product_ID,
        Quantity
   from orion.product_dim as p
        left join
        orion.order_fact as o
        on p.Product_ID=o.Product_ID
```

```
      where Order_ID is missing;
quit;
title;
```

6. Creating a Report with a Self-Join

```
*** s104s06 ***;

proc sql;
title 'Trainee and Temporary Employees';
select a1.Employee_ID 'Employee ID',
        a1.Employee_Name 'Employee_ Name',
        Job_Title,
        a2.Employee_ID 'Manager ID',
        a2.Employee_Name 'Manager Name'
    from orion.employee_addresses as a1,
        orion.employee_addresses as a2,
        orion.staff as s
    where a1.Employee_ID=s.Employee_ID and
          s.Manager_ID=a2.Employee_ID and
          (Job_Title contains 'Trainee' or
           Job_Title contains 'Temp')
    order by a1.Employee_ID;
quit;
title;
```

7. Joining Multiple Tables

```
*** s104s07 ***;

proc sql;
title "Employees With More Than 30 Years of Service";
title2 "As of February 1, 2013";
select emp.Employee_Name 'Employee Name' format=$35.,
        int(('1FEB2013'd-Employee_Hire_Date)/365.25)
            as YOS 'Years of Service',
        mgr.Employee_Name 'Manager Name' as Manager_Name
        /* Employee_Addresses:
           First copy is required to
           look up Employee information Employee's
           Employee_ID */
        /* Employee_Organization:
           Links Employee_ID to Manager_ID */
        /* Employee_Addresses:
           Second copy is required to
           look up Manager information using Manager's
           Employee_ID */
    from orion.employee_addresses as emp,
        orion.employee_organization as org,
        orion.employee_payroll as pay,
        orion.employee_addresses as mgr
    where emp.Employee_ID=pay.Employee_ID
          and emp.Employee_ID=org.Employee_ID
```

```
            and org.Manager_ID=mgr.Employee_ID
            and calculated YOS gt 30
     order by Manager_Name, YOS desc, Employee_Name;
quit;
title;
```

Solutions to Student Activities (Polls/Quizzes)

4.01 Multiple Choice Poll – Correct Answer

Which of these DATA step statements is used to combine tables horizontally?

a. SET
b. APPEND
c. MERGE
d. INPUT
e. INFILE

8

4.02 Quiz – Correct Answer

How many rows and columns are returned from this query?

20 rows

5 columns

ID	Name	ID	Action	Amount
101	Jones	102	Purchase	$376
101	Jones	102	Return	$119
101	Jones	103	Purchase	$57
101	Jones	105	Purchase	$98
101	Jones	102	Purchase	$376
101	Jones	102	Return	$119
101	Jones	103	Purchase	$57
101	Jones	105	Purchase	$98
102	Kent	102	Purchase	$376
102	Kent	102	Return	$119
102	Kent	103	Purchase	$57
102	Kent	105	Purchase	$98
102	Kent	102	Purchase	$376
102	Kent	102	Return	$119
102	Kent	103	Purchase	$57
102	Kent	105	Purchase	$98
104	Avery	102	Purchase	$376
104	Avery	102	Return	$119
104	Avery	103	Purchase	$57
104	Avery	105	Purchase	$98

25

4.03 Quiz – Correct Answer

Why are there two ID columns in the result?

ID	Name	ID	Action	Amount
102	Blank	102	Purchase	$100

The * was used to select all columns from both tables.
Therefore, you have two ID columns in the results.

32

4.04 Quiz – Correct Answer

What message is displayed in the log when the program is executed?

ERROR messages are shown.

```
ERROR: Ambiguous reference, column ID is in more than one table.
ERROR: Ambiguous reference, column ID is in more than one table.
  quit;
NOTE: The SAS System stopped processing this step because of errors.
```

36

4.05 Multiple Choice Poll – Correct Answer

How many rows (observations) result from the DATA step MERGE statement in program **s104a03**?

a. 2
b. 4
c. 6
d. 20
e. none of the above

Obs	ID	Name	Action	Amount
1	102	Kent	Purchase	$376
2	102	Kent	Return	$119

customer2

ID	Name
101	Jones
101	Jones
102	Kent
102	Kent
104	Avery

transaction2

ID	Action	Amount
102	Purchase	$376
102	Return	$119
103	Purchase	$57
105	Purchase	$98

44

4.06 Quiz – Correct Answer

How many tables can be combined using the following PROC SQL syntax?

```
proc sql;
select *
   from table-name,..., table-name
   where sql-expression;
quit;
```

Up to 256 tables can be joined with this syntax.

48

4.07 Quiz – Correct Answer

Given these two SELECT statements:

```
select *
    from customers left join transactions
    on customers.ID=transactions.ID;
```

```
select *
    from transactions right join customers
    on customers.ID=transactions.ID;
```

1. Will the result sets contain the same data? **Yes**
2. What is the difference in the result sets? **The columns are in a different order.**

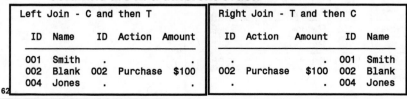

| Left Join - C and then T | | | | | Right Join - T and then C | | | | |
ID	Name	ID	Action	Amount	ID	Action	Amount	ID	Name
001	Smith	.		.	.		.	001	Smith
002	Blank	002	Purchase	$100	002	Purchase	$100	002	Blank
004	Jones	.		.	.		.	004	Jones

62

4.08 Multiple Choice Poll – Correct Answer

For the report, you need the data for all married employees from **orion.employee_payroll**.
You also want to include the charity names from the **orion.employee_donations** table if **Employee_ID** matches. What type of join should you use to combine the information from these two tables?

a. inner join
(b.) left join
c. full join
d. none of the above

69

Chapter 5   Subqueries

5.1 Noncorrelated Subqueries

Objectives

- Define PROC SQL subqueries.
- Differentiate between correlated and noncorrelated subqueries.
- Subset data based on values returned from a subquery.

3

Business Scenario

HR and Payroll managers requested a report that displays **Job_Title** for job groups with an average salary greater than the average salary of the company as a whole.

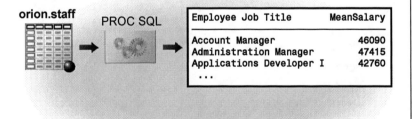

Employee Job Title	MeanSalary
Account Manager	46090
Administration Manager	47415
Applications Developer I	42760
...	

4

Step 1

Calculate the company's average salary.

```
proc sql;
select avg(Salary) as CompanyMeanSalary
    from orion.staff;
quit;
```

Company MeanSalary
38041.51

s105d01

5

Step 2

Determine the job titles whose average salary exceeds the company's average salary.

```
proc sql;
select Job_Title,
       avg(Salary) as MeanSalary
    from orion.staff
    group by Job_Title
    having MeanSalary>38041.51;
quit;
```

Partial PROC SQL Output

Employee Job Title	MeanSalary
Account Manager	46090
Administration Manager	47415
Applications Developer I	42760

s105d01

6

Step 3

Write the program as a single step using a subquery.

A *subquery* is a query that resides within an outer query.

outer query

```
proc sql;
select Job_Title, avg(Salary) as MeanSalary
    from orion.staff
    group by Job_Title
    having avg(Salary) >
        (select avg(Salary)
            from orion.staff);
quit;
```

subquery

✏ The subquery must be resolved before the outer query can be resolved

s105d02

7

Subqueries

A subquery

- returns values to be used in the outer query's WHERE or HAVING clause
- must return only a single column
- can return multiple values or a single value.

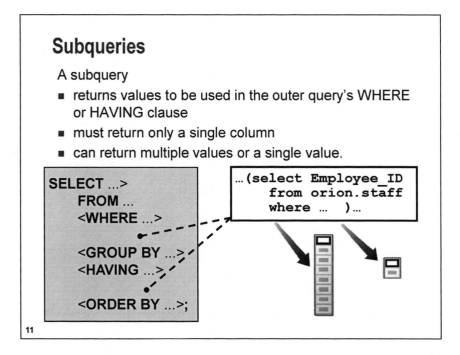

```
SELECT ...>
    FROM ...
    <WHERE ...>

    <GROUP BY ...>
    <HAVING ...>

    <ORDER BY ...>;
```

```
...(select Employee_ID
    from orion.staff
    where ...  )...
```

11

Subqueries are also known as *nested queries*, *inner queries*, and *sub-selects*.

Setup for the Poll

Is the following SELECT statement valid as a subquery?

```
(select Employee_ID,
        Gender
 from orion.staff)
```

12

5.01 Poll

Is the SELECT statement valid as a subquery?

○ Yes
○ No

13

Subqueries: Noncorrelated

There are two types of subqueries:

- A *noncorrelated subquery* is a self-contained query.
  It executes independently of the outer query.

```
proc sql;
select Job_Title, avg(Salary) as MeanSalary
    from orion.staff
    group by Job_Title
    having avg(Salary) >
        (select avg(Salary)
            from orion.staff);
quit;
```

This query is a stand-alone query.

15

Subqueries: Correlated

- A *correlated subquery* requires a value or values to
  be passed to it by the outer (main) query before it
  can be successfully resolved.

```
proc sql;
select Employee_ID, avg(Salary) as MeanSalary
    from orion.employee_addresses
    where 'AU'=
        (select Country
            from work.supervisors
            where employee_addresses.Employee_ID=
                supervisors.Employee_ID);
quit;
```

This query is not stand-alone.
It needs additional information
from the main query.

16

Noncorrelated Subquery

```
proc sql;
select Job_Title,
       avg(Salary) as MeanSalary
  from orion.staff
  group by Job_Title
  having avg(Salary) >
     (select avg(Salary)
        from orion.staff);
quit;
```

Evaluate the subquery first.

18   s105d02

Noncorrelated Subquery

```
proc sql;
select Job_Title,
       avg(Salary) as MeanSalary
  from orion.staff
  group by Job_Title
  having avg(Salary) >
     (38041.51);
quit;
```

Then pass the results to the outer query.

Partial PROC SQL Output

Employee Job Title	MeanSalary
Account Manager	46090
Administration Manager	47415
Applications Developer I	42760

19   s105d02

5.02 Poll

Can a subquery contain a subquery?

○ Yes

○ No

20

Business Scenario

The CEO sends a birthday card to each employee having a birthday in the current month. Create a report listing the names, cities, and countries of employees with February birthdays.

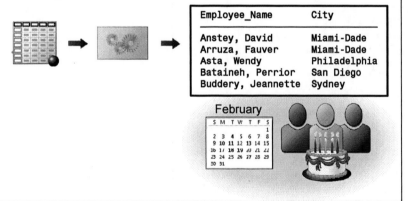

Employee_Name	City
Anstey, David	Miami-Dade
Arruza, Fauver	Miami-Dade
Asta, Wendy	Philadelphia
Bataineh, Perrior	San Diego
Buddery, Jeannette	Sydney

February

S	M	T	W	T	F	S
						1
2	3	4	5	6	7	8
9	10	11	12	13	14	15
16	17	18	19	20	21	22
23	24	25	26	27	28	29
30	31					

22

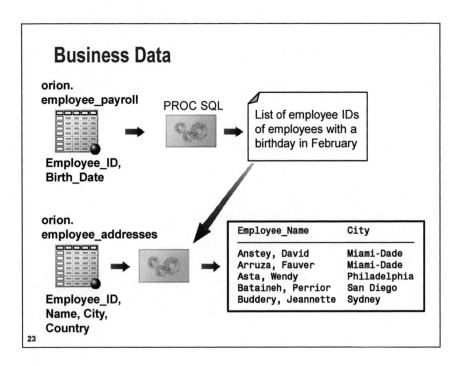

Noncorrelated Subqueries

```
proc sql;
select Employee_Name, City,
       Country
   from orion.employee_addresses
   where Employee_ID in
       (select Employee_ID
           from orion.employee_payroll
           where month(Birth_Date)=2)
   order by Employee_Name;
quit;
```

s105d04

24

To make this code dynamic, replace the month value, *2*, with **month(today())**. Now the program will return a list of employees with a birthday in the current month.

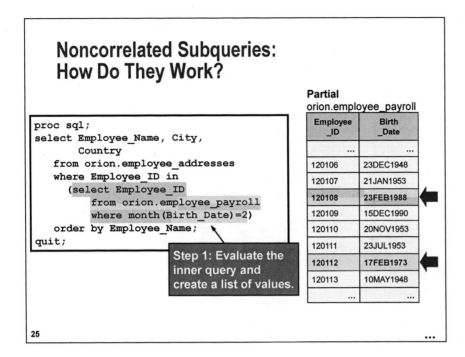

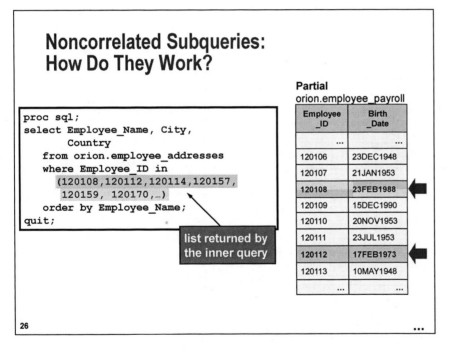

Noncorrelated Subqueries: How Do They Work?

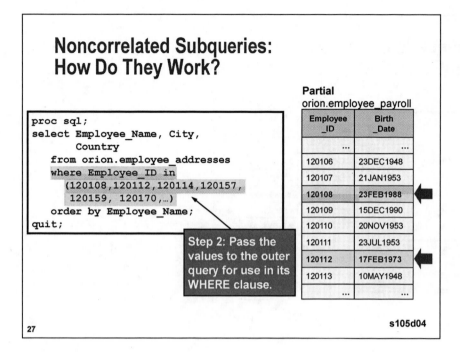

Partial
orion.employee_payroll

Employee _ID	Birth _Date
...	...
120106	23DEC1948
120107	21JAN1953
120108	23FEB1988
120109	15DEC1990
120110	20NOV1953
120111	23JUL1953
120112	17FEB1973
120113	10MAY1948
...	...

```
proc sql;
select Employee_Name, City,
       Country
   from orion.employee_addresses
   where Employee_ID in
       (120108,120112,120114,120157,
        120159, 120170,…)
   order by Employee_Name;
quit;
```

Step 2: Pass the values to the outer query for use in its WHERE clause.

27   s105d04

Viewing the Output

Partial PROC SQL Output

Employee_Name	City	Country
Anstey, David	Miami-Dade	US
Arruza, Fauver	Miami-Dade	US
Asta, Wendy	Philadelphia	US
Bataineh, Perrior	San Diego	US
Buddery, Jeannette	Sydney	AU

28

Setup for the Poll

- Open the program **s105a01**.
- Change the IN operator to an equal sign in the code.
- Run the changed program and review the SAS log for messages.

```
proc sql;
select Employee_Name, City, Country
   from orion.employee_addresses
   where Employee_ID =
      (select Employee_ID
          from orion.employee_payroll
          where month(Birth_Date)=2)
   order by 1;
quit;
```

29

5.03 Multiple Choice Poll

What happens when you change the comparison operator to an equal sign?

a. Nothing special, the program runs fine.

b. You get multiple rows returned in your output.

c. You get an error message.

d. a and b

30

Subqueries That Return Multiple Values

When a subquery returns multiple values and the EQUAL operator is used, an ERROR message is generated.

```
ERROR: Subquery evaluated to more than one row.
```

🖊 If the subquery returns multiple values, you must use the IN operator or a comparison operator with the ANY or ALL keywords.

32

ANY Keyword

The ANY expression is true if it is true for any of the values returned by the subquery.

Keyword ANY	Signifies...
= ANY(20,30,40)	=20 or =30 or =40
> ANY(20,30,40)	> 20
< ANY(20,30,40)	< 40

🖊 The values 20,30,40 represent values returned from a subquery.

33

ALL Keyword

The ALL expression is true if it is true for all the values returned by the subquery.

Keyword ALL	Signifies
> ALL(20,30,40)	> 40
< ALL(20,30,40)	< 20

✏ The values 20,30,40 represent values returned from a subquery.

34

Business Scenario

The senior sales executive asked the following: "Do any Level IV sales representatives have a salary that is lower than any of the lower-level sales representatives?"

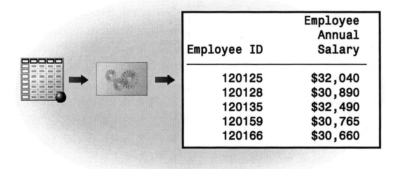

Employee ID	Employee Annual Salary
120125	$32,040
120128	$30,890
120135	$32,490
120159	$30,765
120166	$30,660

35

Solution 1: ANY Keyword

```
proc sql;
select Employee_ID, Salary
    from orion.staff
    where Job_Title='Sales Rep. IV'
          and Salary < any
      (select Salary
          from orion.staff
          where Job_Title in
                ('Sales Rep. I','Sales Rep. II',
                'Sales Rep. III'));
quit;
```

36   s105d05

Solution 2: MAX Statistic

```
proc sql;
select Employee_ID, Salary
    from orion.staff
    where Job_Title='Sales Rep. IV'
          and Salary <
      (select max(Salary)
          from orion.staff
          where Job_Title in
                ('Sales Rep. I','Sales Rep. II',
                'Sales Rep. III'));
quit;
```

37   s105d05

Viewing the Output

Partial PROC SQL Output

```
Level IV Sales Reps Who Earn Less Than
     Any Lower Level Sales Reps.

                        Employee
                          Annual
         Employee ID      Salary
         _____

             120125      $32,040
             120128      $30,890
             120135      $32,490
             120159      $30,765
             120166      $30,660
```

38

Exercises

If you restarted your SAS session since the last exercise, open and submit the **libname.sas** program found in the data folder.

Level 1

1. **Using a Noncorrelated Subquery**

   The **orion.order_fact** table contains information about orders that were placed by customers. Create a report that lists the retail customers whose average retail price exceeds the company average retail sales.

   a. Write a query that displays the average of **Total_Retail_Sales** for all retail sales in the table.

   - Use **AVG(Total_Retail_Sales)** to calculate the average.

   - Subset the rows so that only the retail sales are included (**Order_Type**=*1*).

   PROC SQL Output

MeanSales
137.8227

   b. Write a query that displays **Customer_ID** and **AVG(Total_Retail_Sales)** for those customers whose average retail sales exceed the company average retail sales. The query should do the following:

   - Display the values for **Customer_ID** and **AVG(Total_Retail_Sales)**. Name the second column **MeanSales**.

- Subset the rows do only the retail sales are included (**Order_Type**=*1*).
- Group the data by **Customer_ID**.
- Include only groups where the employee's average quantity of items sold exceeds the company average. Use the query from **1.a.** as a subquery in the HAVING clause.
- Add a title to the report as shown.

Partial PROC SQL Output

```
              Customers Whose Average Retail Sales
               Exceeds the Average Retail Sales
                       for All Customers

               Customer ID   MeanSales
               _____

                       10      141.91
                       17      139.03
                       31      158.11
                       45      178.03
                       49      161.66
```

Level 2

2. **Using a Noncorrelated Subquery**

   Each month a memo is posted that lists the employees who have employment anniversaries for that month. Create the report for the current month and list **Employee_ID** and the first and last names for all employees hired during the current month of any year.

   You can find **Employee_Name** in the **orion.employee_addresses** table and **Employee_Hire_Date** in the **orion.employee_payroll** table. Both tables contain the column **Employee_ID**. Order the report by an employee's last name.

   a. Create a query that returns a list of employee IDs for employees with a current anniversary. The query should do the following:

   - Display **Employee_ID** numbers.
   - Use the **orion.employee_payroll** table.
   - Return only employees whose hire date (**Employee_Hire_Date**) is in in the current month.
   - Add a title to the report as shown.

   Partial PROC SQL Output (Generated when current month = February)

```
          Employee IDs for Current Month Anniversaries

                        Employee_ID
                        _____

                          120107
                          120116
                          120136
                          120162
                          120164
```

   b. Using the query in **2.a.** as a noncorrelated subquery, write a query that displays the employee IDs and names of employees who have current month anniversaries. The final query should do the following:

- Display **Employee_ID** and split **Employee_Name** into two new columns: **FirstName** and **LastName**. Both new columns should have a length of $15 and appropriate labels. (See the report below.) The original **Employee_Name** is stored as **Lastname, Firstname**.
- Use the **orion.employee_addresses** table.
- Select **Employee_ID** only for employees who had current month anniversaries.
- Order the final results by **LastName**.
- Create an appropriate title.

Partial PROC SQL Output (Generated when current month = February)

```
              Employees with Current Month Anniversaries

          Employee_ID  First Name      Last Name
          _____

               121030  Jeryl           Areu
               121007  John            Banaszak
               120667  Edwin           Droste
               120778  Angela          Gardner
```

3. **Creating Subqueries Using the ALL Keyword**

   In most companies, you can assume that the higher-level job titles have employees that are older than employees with a lower-level job title. Using the **orion.staff** table, determine whether there are any lower-level purchasing agents (Purchasing Agent I and Purchasing Agent II) that are older than all the higher-level purchasing agents (Purchasing Agent III). The final report should display **Employee_ID**, **Job_Title**, **Birth_Date**, and a calculated **Age** column for the employee as of 02FEB2013.

   Hint: Use the SAS date constant (**'02FEB2013'd**) in the calculation for **Age**. If you use the TODAY function to calculate the age, the values will differ from the results below:

```
                     Level I or II Purchasing Agents
                  Who are older than ALL Purchasing Agent IIIs

                                                Employee
                                                   Birth
            Employee ID  Employee Job Title         Date     Age
            _____

                 120742  Purchasing Agent I      04FEB1948    64
```

Challenge

4. **Using Nested Subqueries**

   The Marketing Department is interested in developing a campaign pointed toward the Orion Club members low activity group. They specifically want to identify the customer IDs of this group whose last order was placed before 1Jan20112. The requested report should contain the customer ID and the date of the customer's last order.

   The following tables contain the data that you need:

   orion.customer_type contains the columns **Customer_Type** and **Customer_Type_ID**

   orion.customer contains **Customer_Type_ID** and **Customer_ID**

   orion.order_fact contains **Customer_ID** and **Order_Date**.

PROC SQL Output

```
                  Latest Order Date for
             Orion Club Low Activity Members

             Customer ID    Order Date

                        4   18-DEC-2008
                       18   16-FEB-2011
                       34   18-NOV-2011
                       65   03-AUG-2011
                       69   18-OCT-2011
                       75   10-NOV-2008
                       92   01-MAY-2011
                      183   21-APR-2011
                      195   12-JUN-2010
                      928   04-SEP-2011
                     1033   06-MAY-2011
                     1100   10-DEC-2010
                     1684   01-AUG-2010
                    70046   05-FEB-2008
                    70108   22-JUL-2009
                    70165   28-JUL-2011
```

5.2 In-Line Views

Objectives

- Create and use in-line views.
- Use in-line views and subqueries to simplify coding a complex query.

42

Business Scenario

List all active Sales Department employees who have annual salaries significantly lower (less than 95%) than the average salary for everyone with the same job title.

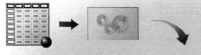

```
            Employees with Salaries less than
              95% of the Average for their Job

                                      Employee
                                        Annual
   Employee_Name      Employee Job Title  Salary   Job_Avg

   Ould, Tulsidas     Sales Rep. I       22,710   26,576
   Polky, Asishana    Sales Rep. I       25,110   26,576
   Voron, Tachaun     Sales Rep. I       25,125   26,576
```

43

Step 1

Calculate the average salaries for active employees in the Sales Department, grouped by job title.

```
title  'Sales Department Average Salary';
title2 'By Job Title';
select Job_Title,
       avg(Salary) as Job_Avg
  from orion.employee_payroll as p,
       orion.employee_organization as o
  where p.Employee_ID=o.Employee_ID
        and Employee_Term_Date is missing
        and Department="Sales"
  group by Job_Title;
```

44   s105d06

Viewing the Output

PROC SQL Output

```
            Sales Department Average Salary
                      by Job Title

        Job_Title                    Job_Avg
        _____

        Sales Rep. I                26575.76
        Sales Rep. II               27347.97
        Sales Rep. III              29213.62
        Sales Rep. IV                31588.5
```

Setup for the Poll

Can this SELECT statement be used as a subquery?

```
select Job_Title,
       avg(Salary) as Job_Avg
       format=comma7.
  from orion.employee_payroll as p,
       orion.employee_organization as o
  where p.Employee_ID=o.Employee_ID
        and Employee_Term_Date is missing
        and Department="Sales"
  group by Job_Title;
```

5.04 Poll

Can this SELECT statement be used as a subquery?

○ Yes
○ No

47

In-Line Views

An *in-line view* is a query expression (SELECT statement) that resides in a FROM clause. It acts as a virtual table, used in place of a physical table in a query.

```
PROC SQL;
SELECT *
  FROM
    (in-line view query expression)
    ...;
QUIT;
```

In-line views are often useful when you build complex SQL queries.

49

✎   An in-line view consists of any valid SQL query, except that it must not contain an ORDER BY clause. In-line views can be independently tested while building a complex query, which can simplify troubleshooting.

Step 2

Match each employee to a job title group and compare the employee's salary to the group's average to determine whether it is less than 95% of the group average.

```
select Employee_Name, emp.Job_Title,
       Salary format=comma7., Job_Avg format=comma7.
  from (select Job_Title,
               avg(Salary) as Job_Avg format=comma7.
          from orion.employee_payroll as p,
               orion.employee_organization as o
         where p.Employee_ID=o.Employee_ID
           and Employee_Term_Date is missing
           and Department="Sales"
         group by Job_Title) as job,
       orion.salesstaff as emp
 where emp.Job_Title=job.Job_Title
   and Salary<Job_Avg*.95
   and Emp_Term_Date is missing
 order by Job_Title, Employee_Name;
```

50   s105d07

✎   You can assign an alias to an in-line view as if it were a table.

Viewing the Output

PROC SQL Output

Employees with Salaries less than 95% of the Average for their Job			
Employee_Name	Employee Job Title	Employee Annual Salary	Job_Avg
Ould, Tulsidas	Sales Rep. I	22,710	26,576
Polky, Asishana	Sales Rep. I	25,110	26,576
Voron, Tachaun	Sales Rep. I	25,125	26,576

51

Setup for the Poll

```
select Name, emp.Job_Title, Job_Avg
   from (in-line view) as job,
        orion.staff as emp
   where emp.Job_Title=job.Job_Title;
select Job_Title, Job_Avg
   from job;
```

The first SELECT statement uses an in-line view to create data that is referenced with the alias **job**. Can **job** also be referenced in the second SELECT statement?

52

5.05 Poll

The first SELECT statement uses an in-line view to create data that is referenced with the alias **job**. Can **job** also be referenced in the second SELECT statement?

○ Yes
○ No

53

Business Scenario

Management wants to incent more sales of Expedition Zero sleeping bags by rewarding each sales associate who sold these items in 2011 with a $50 certificate.

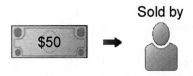

Sold by

The Task:
Prepare a list of the managers' names and cities for those employees who qualify for the certificate.

56

Business Data

Because this query involves four tables, it might not be easy to code all at once. To simplify the task, split the query into small parts. Test each part individually, and test the overall query each time that a new segment is added.

These tables are required for this query:

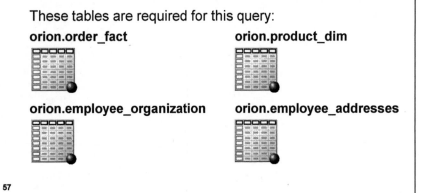

orion.order_fact

orion.product_dim

orion.employee_organization

orion.employee_addresses

57

Planning the Complex Query

This query involves multiple tables. To simplify the task, split the query into parts and test as you progress.

| Part 1 | Identify the employees who sold Expedition Zero merchandise in 2011. |

| Part 2 | Find the employee identifier for the managers of these employees. |

| Part 3 | Obtain the managers' names and city information. |

58

Business Data: Part 1

| Part 1 | Get employee IDs for employees who sold Expedition Zero merchandise in 2011. |

Select the employee's identifier (**Employee_ID**) from the results of joining the **order_fact** and **product_dim** tables on **Product_ID**, where **Product_Name** contains *Expedition Zero*. Exclude Internet and catalog orders (**Employee_ID NE 99999999**).

59

Coding the Complex Query

Part 1 Write a query to obtain the employee ID of all employees who sold Expedition Zero merchandise in 2011.

```
select distinct Employee_ID
   from orion.order_fact as of,
        orion.product_dim as p
   where of.Product_ID=p.Product_ID
         and year(Order_Date)=2011
         and Product_Name contains
         'Expedition Zero'
         and Employee_ID ne 99999999;
```

PROC SQL Output

Employee ID
121065

60   s105d08

Business Data: Part 2

Part 2 Find the employee identifier for the managers of these employees.

Select the manager's identifier (**Manager_ID**) from the results of joining the **employee_organization** table with the first query's results on **Employee_ID**.

61

Setup for the Poll

To join the **employee_organization** table with the Step 1 query results, you use the query from Step 1 as which of the following?

```
select distinct Employee_ID
   from orion.order_fact as of,
        orion.product_dim as p
   where of.Product_ID=p.Product_ID
         and year(Order_Date)=2011
         and Product_Name contains
         'Expedition Zero'
         and Employee_ID ne 99999999;
```

62

5.06 Multiple Choice Poll

To join the **employee_organization** table with the Step 1 query results, you use the query from Step 1 as which of the following?

a. an in-line view
b. a noncorrelated subquery
c. either a or b
d. neither a or b

63

Coding the Complex Query

Part 2 Write a query to obtain the manager ID
of the employee's manager.

```
select Manager_ID
   from orion.employee_organization as o,
      (<Step 1 query results>) as ID
   where o.Employee_ID=ID.Employee_ID;
```

```
Employee_ID
   121065
```

65

Coding the Complex Query

Part 2 Write a query to obtain the manager ID
of the employee's manager.

```
select Manager_ID
   from orion.employee_organization as o,
      (select distinct Employee_ID
         from orion.order_fact as of,
            orion.product_dim as p
         where of.Product_ID=p.Product_ID
            and year(Order_Date)=2011
            and Product_Name
            contains 'Expedition Zero'
            and Employee_ID ne 99999999)as ID
   where o.Employee_ID=ID.Employee_ID;
```

PROC SQL Output

```
Manager_ID
   121145
```

66

s105d09

Business Data: Part 3

Part 3 Find the managers' names and cities.

Select the employee's name (**Employee_Name**) and city from the **employee_addresses** table, where **Employee_ID** matches **Manager_ID** in the results of the previous query.

67

Setup for the Poll

Is it possible to use the entire query in Step 2 as a subquery?

```
select Manager_ID
   from orion.employee_organization as o,
      (select distinct Employee_ID
          from orion.order_fact as of,
              orion.product_dim as p
         where of.Product_ID=p.Product_ID
             and year(Order_Date)=2007
             and Product_Name
             contains 'Expedition Zero'
             and Employee_ID ne 99999999)as ID
   where o.Employee_ID=ID.Employee_ID;
```

68

5.07 Poll

Is it possible to use the entire query in Step 2 as a subquery?

O Yes

O No

69

Coding the Complex Query

Part 3 Write a query to obtain the managers' names and city information.

```
proc sql;
select Employee_Name format=$25. as Name, City
   from orion.employee_addresses
   where Employee_ID in
       (<Step 2 query results>);
```

Manager_ID
121145

71

Coding the Complex Query

```
proc sql;
select Employee_Name format=$25. as Name, City
   from orion.employee_addresses
   where Employee_ID in
        (select Manager_ID
            from orion.employee_organization as o,
            (select distinct Employee_ID
                from orion.order_fact as of,
                     orion.product_dim as p
                where of.Product_ID=p.Product_ID
                and year(Order_Date)=2011
                and Product_Name contains
                    'Expedition Zero'
                and Employee_ID ne 99999999) as ID
            where o.Employee_ID=ID.Employee_ID);
```

Part 3

s105d10

72

Viewing the Output

Part 3

PROC SQL Output

Name	City
Lansberry, Dennis	Miami-Dade

73

Coding the Complex Query

You can also solve this problem using a multiway join.

```
proc sql;
select distinct Employee_Name format=$25. as Name, City
   from orion.order_fact as of,
        orion.product_dim as pd,
        orion.employee_organization as eo,
        orion.employee_addresses as ea
   where of.Product_ID=pd.Product_ID
         and of.Employee_ID=eo.Employee_ID
         and ea.Employee_ID=eo.Manager_ID
         and Product_Name contains 'Expedition Zero'
         and year(Order_Date)=2011
         and eo.Employee_ID ne 99999999;
quit;
```

74   s105d11

Comparison with Traditional SAS Programs

```
*** s105d12 ***;

   /* Traditional SAS Program Code */
   /* for Complex Join            */

   /********************************************************
   Step 1:  Identify the employees who sold Expedition Zero
            merchandise in 2003.
   ********************************************************/
proc sort data=orion.order_fact
            (keep=Product_ID Employee_ID Order_Date
            where=(YEAR(Order_Date)=2011 and Employee_ID ne 99999999))
            out=orders_2011 (Drop=Order_Date);
   by Product_ID;
run;
proc sort data=orion.product_dim (keep=Product_ID Product_Name)
            out=products;
   by Product_ID;
run;
data employees (Keep=Employee_ID);
   merge orders_2011 (In=KeepMe)
         products (where=(Product_Name contains 'Expedition Zero'));
   by Product_ID;
   if KeepMe and Product_Name ne '';
run;

proc sort data=employees nodup;
   by Employee_ID;
run;
```

```
   /*********************************************************
   Step 2:   Find the employee identifier for the managers of
             these employees
   *********************************************************/
data manager_id (rename=(Manager_ID=Employee_ID));
   merge employees (in=KeepMe)
         orion.employee_organization (keep=Employee_ID Manager_ID);
   by Employee_ID;
   if KeepMe;
   drop Employee_ID;
run;
proc sort data=manager_id nodup;
   by Employee_ID;
run;

   /*********************************************************
   Step 3:   Obtain the managers' names and city information
   *********************************************************/
proc sort data=orion.employee_addresses (Keep=Employee_ID
Employee_Name City)
         out=employees;
   by Employee_ID;
run;

data managers;
   length Manager $28.;
   merge manager_id (in=KeepMe)
         employees;
   by Employee_ID;
   if KeepMe;
   Manager=catx(' ',scan(Employee_Name,2,','),
           scan(Employee_Name,1,','));
   drop Employee_ID Employee_Name;
run;
proc print data=managers noobs;
run;
```

Exercises

If you restarted your SAS session since the last exercise, open and submit the **libname.sas** program found in the data folder.

Level 1

5. Using In-Line Views

Produce a report of Orion Star sales force employees' aggregate sales in 2011.

a. Select **Country**, **First_Name**, **Last_Name**, **Value_Sold**, **Orders**, and **Avg_Order** columns by joining **orion.order_fact** and **orion.sales** tables on **Employee_ID**. Group the report by **Country**,

First_Name, Last_Name. Include only employees having an aggregate **Value_Sold** of $200.00 or more. Order the results by **Country**, **Value_Sold** (descending), and **Orders** (descending).

- Calculate Value_Sold by summing Total_Retail_Price.
- Calculate Orders by using the COUNT(*) function to count the number of rows returned for each employee.
- Calculate Avg_Order by dividing Value_Sold by Orders.
- Title the report as indicated in the sample output.

Partial PROC SQL Output

```
                       2011 Sales Force Sales Statistics
                     For Employees With $200.00 or More In Sales


        Country   First_Name    Last_Name          Value_Sold   Orders  Avg_Order
       ─────────────────────────────────────────────────────────────────────────

        AU        Lucian        Daymond                880.10        5     176.02
        AU        Ranj          Stamalis               697.60        3     232.53
        AU        Sharryn       Clarkson               400.40        3     133.47
        AU        Marinus       Surawski               398.80        2     199.40
        AU        Sian          Shannan                306.20        1     306.20
        AU        Monica        Kletschkus             239.30        2     119.65
        US        Tywanna       Mcdade               1,387.90        2     693.95
```

b. Rewrite the query created in **a** and use it as an in-line view. Select **Country**, the maximum **Value_Sold**, **Orders**, and **Avg_Order** as well as the minimum **Avg_Order** for each country. Name the report **2011 Sales Summary by Country**.

Hint: An in-line view must not use the ORDER BY clause.

PROC SQL Output

```
                      2011 Sales Summary by Country


                     Max Value     Max      Max      Min
            Country       Sold   Orders  Average  Average
           ──────────────────────────────────────────────

            AU          880.10     5.00   306.20   119.65
            US        1,387.90     6.00   693.95    66.50
```

Level 2

6. **Building Complex Queries with In-Line Views**

Your ultimate goal in this exercise is to create a report showing each employee's salary expressed as a percentage of the total salary for that employee's department. The report should be sorted by department and, within each department, in descending order of salary percentage.

- The **orion.employee_payroll** table contains **Salary**.
- The **orion.employee_addresses** table contains **Employee_Name**.
- The **orion.employee_organization** table contains **Department**.

Sketch of desired report:

```
┌──────────────────────────────────────────────────────────────────┐
│                                                                    │
│        Employee Salaries as a percent of Department Total          │
│                                                                    │
└──────────────────────────────────────────────────────────────────┘
```

Department	Employee_Name	Salary	Percent
Accounts	Mea, Azavious	58,200.00	8.6%
Accounts	Miller, Pamela	53,475.00	7.9%
Accounts	Asta, Wendy	52,295.00	7.7%

a. Create a report aggregating the sum of all salaries for each department. The report should include **Department** and the sum of all associated salary values as **Dept_Salary_Total**. Join **orion.employee_payroll** and **orion.employee_organization** by **Employee_ID** to obtain the information you need.

- The **orion.employee_payroll** table contains salary values.

- The **orion.employee_organization** table contains department information.

Partial PROC SQL Output

```
                                        Dept_Salary_
        Department                             Total
        _____

        Accounts                              680440
        Accounts Management                   397175
        Administration                       1009850
        Concession Management                 372225
        Engineering                           276285
```

b. Create a report that includes the employee ID, name, and department. Join **orion.employee_addresses** and **orion.employee_organization** by **Employee_ID** to obtain the information you need.

- The **orion.employee_addresses** table contains **Employee_Name** and **Employee_ID**.

- The **orion.employee_organization** table contains **Employee_ID** and **Department**.

Partial PROC SQL Output

```
Employee_
     ID  Employee_Name               Department
     _____

  121044  Abbott, Ray                 Sales
  120145  Aisbitt, Sandy              Sales
  120761  Akinfolarin, Tameaka        Accounts
  120656  Amos, Salley                Logistics Management
  121107  Anger, Rose                 Sales
  121038  Anstey, David               Sales
```

c. Use the two queries that you created in **a** and **b** as in-line views. Join the views with **orion.employee_payroll** by either **Employee_ID** or **Department** to create the final report.

- The query from step **a** contains **Department** and **Dept_Salary_Total**.

- The query from step **b** contains **Employee_ID**, **Employee_Name**, and **Department**.

- The **orion.employee_payroll** table contains **Employee_ID** and individual **Salary** values.

Partial PROC SQL Output

```
            Employee Salaries as a percent of Department Total

    Department                  Employee_Name               Salary  Percent
    _____
```

Accounts		Mea, Azavious	58,200.00	8.6%
Accounts		Miller, Pamela	53,475.00	7.9%
Accounts		Asta, Wendy	52,295.00	7.7%
Accounts		Post, Nahliah	48,380.00	7.1%
Accounts		Ferrari, Ralph	47,000.00	6.9%
Accounts		Kimmerle, Kevie	46,090.00	6.8%
Accounts		Farthing, Zashia	43,590.00	6.4%
Accounts		Knopfmacher, Paul	38,545.00	5.7%
Accounts		Thoits, Elizabeth	36,440.00	5.4%
Accounts		Apr, Nishan	36,230.00	5.3%
Accounts		Atkins, John	34,760.00	5.1%
Accounts		Voltz, Sal	34,040.00	5.0%
Accounts		Woods, Connie	32,675.00	4.8%
Accounts		Akinfolarin, Tameaka	30,960.00	4.5%
Accounts		Leone, Marvin	30,625.00	4.5%
Accounts		Van Damme, Jean-Claude	30,590.00	4.5%
Accounts		Niemann, Kevin	26,545.00	3.9%
Accounts Management		Kempster, Janelle	53,400.00	13%
Accounts Management		Kokoszka, Nikeisha	51,950.00	13%
Accounts Management		Lightbourne, Abelino	47,990.00	12%

Challenge

7. **Building a Complex Query Using a Multi-Way Join**

   Create a report using a multi-way inner join, which produces the total of the 2011 sales figures for each Orion Star employee. The report should be titled **2011 Total Sales Figures** and must include both the managers' and employees' names (displayed as first name followed by last name), and the total retail value of all sales made by each employee in 2011. Present the information as follows:

   - Use one row per employee.
   - Organize the report so that the following standards are observed:
     – Employees under one manager are adjacent to each other (grouped together) on the report.
     – Within each manager's group, employees are listed in decreasing order of total sales.
     – The Australian groups are listed first, followed by the U.S. groups.
     – Manager names are in alphabetical order by last name and then first name.

   Remember that you can group and order by columns that are not included in the SELECT statement list.

   The data that you need can be found in the following tables (variables of interest in parentheses):

   - **orion.order_fact (Employee_ID, Total_Retail_Price)**
   - **orion.employee_organization (Employee_ID, Manager_ID)**
   - **orion.employee_addresses (Employee_ID, Employee_Name)**

   Partial PROC SQL Output

2011 Total Sales Figures		
Manager	Employee	Total_Sales
Wilson Dawes	Jina Fiocca	223.80
Wilson Dawes	Phu Sloey	17.60
Wilson Dawes	Amanda Liebman	6.40

Tom Zhou	Lucian Daymond	880.10
Tom Zhou	Ranj Stamalis	697.60
Tom Zhou	Sharryn Clarkson	400.40
Tom Zhou	Marinus Surawski	398.80
Tom Zhou	Sian Shannan	306.20
Tom Zhou	Monica Kletschkus	239.30
Tom Zhou	Fancine Kaiser	147.10
Tom Zhou	Shani Duckett	101.50
Tom Zhou	Atul Leyden	92.50
Tom Zhou	Kevin Lyon	73.99
Tom Zhou	Andrew Conolly	60.80
Tom Zhou	Sean Dives	19.10
Tom Zhou	Lynelle Phoumirath	19.10
Renee Capachietti	Brienne Darrohn	533.40
Renee Capachietti	Michael Westlund	366.00

5.3 Solutions

Solutions to Exercises

1. **Using a Noncorrelated Subquery**

   a.

```
*** s105s01 ***;
/* a */

title;
proc sql;
select avg(Total_Retail_Price) as MeanSales
    from orion.order_fact
    where Order_Type=1;
quit;
```

   b.

```
/* b */

title "Customers Whose Average Retail Sales";
title2 "Exceeds the Average Retail Sales;
title3 "for All Retail Customers";
proc sql;
select Customer_ID,
       avg(Total_Retail_Sales) as MeanSales format=8.2
    from orion.order_fact
    where Order_Type=1
    group by Customer_ID
    having MeanSales >
        (select avg(Total_Retail_Sales)
            from orion.order_fact
            where Order_Type=1);
quit;
title;
```

2. Using a Noncorrelated Subquery

a.

```
*** s105s02***;
/* a */

proc sql;
title "Employee IDs for Current Month Anniversaries";
select Employee_ID
   from orion.employee_payroll
   where month(Employee_Hire_Date)=month(today());
quit;
title;
```

b.

```
/* b */

proc sql;
title "Employees with Current Month Anniversaries";
select  Employee_ID,
        scan(Employee_name,2,', ') format=$15.
           as FirstName 'First Name',
        scan(Employee_name,1,', ') format=$15.
           as LastName 'Last Name'
   from orion.employee_addresses
   where Employee_ID in
      (select Employee_ID
          from orion.employee_payroll
          where month(Employee_Hire_Date)=month(today()))
   order by LastName;
quit;
title;
```

3. Creating Subqueries Using the ALL Keyword

```
*** s105s03***;

proc sql;
title "Level I or II Purchasing Agents";
title2 "Who are older than ALL Purchasing Agent IIIs";
select Employee_ID, Job_Title, Birth_Date,
        int(('02Feb2013'd-Birth_Date)/365.25) as Age
   from orion.staff
   where Job_Title  in ('Purchasing Agent I',
                        'Purchasing Agent II')
      and Birth_Date < all
             (select Birth_Date
                 from orion.staff
                 where Job_Title='Purchasing Agent III');
quit;
title;
```

Alternate Solution

```
proc sql;
```

```
title "Level I or II Purchasing Agents";
title2 "Who are older than ALL Purchasing Agent IIIs";
select Employee_ID, Job_Title, Birth_Date,
       int(('02Feb2013'd-Birth_Date)/365.25) as Age
   from orion.staff
   where Job_Title  in ('Purchasing Agent I',
                          'Purchasing Agent II')
     and Birth_Date <
           (select min(Birth_Date)
               from orion.staff
               where Job_Title='Purchasing Agent III');
quit;
title;
```

4. Using Nested Subqueries

```
*** s105s04 ***;

title 'Latest Order Date for';
title2 'Orion Club Low Activity Members';
proc sql;
select distinct Customer_ID,
       max(Order_Date) 'Order Date' format=date11.
   from orion.order_fact
   where Order_Date < '01Jan2012'd and
         Customer_ID in (
             select Customer_ID
                from orion.customer
                where Customer_Type_ID =
                    (select Customer_Type_ID
                            from orion.customer_type
                            where Customer_Type =
                      'Orion Club members low activity'))
   group by Customer_ID;
quit;
title;
```

Alternate Solution

```
title 'Inner Join with In-Line View';
proc sql;
select c.Customer_ID,
       Date
   from orion.customer_type as t,
        orion.customer as c,
        (select Customer_ID, max(Order_Date) format=date11. as Date
            from orion.order_fact
            where Order_Date < '01JAN2012'd
            group by 1) as of
   where t.Customer_Type_ID=c.Customer_Type_ID
     and c.Customer_ID=of.Customer_ID
     and Customer_Type='Orion Club members low activity';
quit;
title;
```

5. Using In-Line Views

a.

```
*** s105s05 ***;

 /* Summarizing by employee */
proc sql;
title "2011 Sales Force Sales Statistics";
title2 "For Employees With $200.00 or More in Sales";
select Country, First_Name, Last_Name,
       sum(Total_Retail_Price) as Value_Sold format=comma9.2,
       count(*) as Orders,
       calculated Value_Sold / calculated Orders as Avg_Order
           format=comma7.2
   from orion.Order_Fact as of,
        orion.Sales as s
   where of.Employee_ID=s.Employee_ID
         and year(Order_Date)=2011
   group by Country, First_Name, Last_Name
   having Value_Sold ge 200
   order by Country, Value_Sold desc, Orders desc;
quit;
```

b.

```
  /*  Further summarize by country using
      the query from part a. as an in-line view */
proc sql;
title "2011 Sales Summary by Country";
select Country,
       max(Value_Sold) 'Max Value Sold' format=comma9.2,
       max(Orders) 'Max Orders' format=comma7.2,
       max(Avg_Order) 'Max Average' format=comma7.2,
       min(Avg_Order) 'Min Average' format=comma7.2
        /* Begin in-line view */
   from (select Country, First_Name, Last_Name,
                sum(Total_Retail_Price) as Value_Sold,
                count(*) as Orders,
                calculated Value_Sold / calculated Orders
                    as Avg_Order
            from orion.order_fact as of,
                 orion.sales as s
            where of.Employee_ID=s.Employee_ID
                and year(Order_Date)=2011
            group by Country, First_Name, Last_Name
            having Value_Sold ge 200) /* End in-line view */
   group by Country
   order by Country;
quit;
title;
```

6. Building Complex Queries with In-Line Views

a.

```
*** s105s06 ***;

proc sql;
select Department, sum(Salary) as Dept_Salary_Total
   from orion.employee_payroll as pay,
         orion.employee_organization as org
   where org.Employee_ID=pay.Employee_ID
   group by Department;
quit;
```

b.

```
proc sql;
select adr.Employee_ID, Employee_Name, org.Department
   from orion.employee_addresses as adr,
         orion.employee_organization as org
   where adr.Employee_ID=org.Employee_ID;
quit;
```

c.

```
proc sql;
title "Employee Salaries as a Percent of Department Total";
select emp.Department format=$22.,
       emp.Employee_Name format=$28.,
       Salary format=comma9.2,
       Salary/Dept_Salary_Total as Percent
       format=percent6.2
   from orion.employee_payroll as pay,
     /* In-line View: Employee ID, name and department */
        (select adr.Employee_ID, Employee_Name,
                org.Department
            from orion.employee_addresses as adr,
                 orion.employee_organization as org
          where adr.Employee_ID=org.Employee_ID)
          as emp,
     /* In-line View: Aggregate sum of salary by department */
        (select Department, sum(Salary) as Dept_Salary_Total
            from orion.employee_payroll as pay,
                 orion.employee_organization as org
          where org.Employee_ID=pay.Employee_ID
          group by Department)
          as sum
   where sum.Department=emp.Department and
         pay.Employee_ID=emp.Employee_ID
   order by Department, Percent desc;
quit;
```

7. **Building a Complex Query Using a Multi-Way Join**

```
*** s105s07 ***;

proc sql;
```

```
title "2011 Total Sales Figures";
select catx(' ',scan(mgr.Employee_Name,2,','),
            scan(mgr.Employee_Name,1,',')) format=$27.
       as Manager,
       catx(' ',scan(emp.Employee_Name,2,','),
            scan(emp.Employee_Name,1,',')) format=$27.
       as Employee,
       Sum(Total_Retail_Price) format=comma9.2
       as Total_Sales
   from orion.order_fact as order,
        orion.employee_organization as org,
        orion.employee_addresses as emp,
        orion.employee_addresses as mgr
   where order.Employee_ID=org.Employee_ID
     and order.Employee_ID=emp.Employee_ID
     and mgr.Employee_ID=org.Manager_ID
     and year(Order_Date)=2011
     and order.Employee_ID ne 99999999
   group by mgr.Country, mgr.Employee_Name, emp.Employee_Name
   order by mgr.Country, mgr.Employee_Name, Total_Sales desc;
quit;
title;
```

Solutions to Student Activities (Polls/Quizzes)

5.01 Poll – Correct Answer

Is the SELECT statement valid as a subquery?

○ Yes
◉ No

A subquery must return only values in a single column.

14

5.02 Poll – Correct Answer

Can a subquery contain a subquery?

⊙ Yes
○ No

```
title 'Latest Order Date for';
title2 'Orion Club Low Activity Members';
proc sql;
select Customer_ID,
       max(Order_Date) 'Order Date' format=date11.
   from orion.order_fact
   where Order_Date < '1Jan2010'd and
         Customer_ID in
            (select Customer_ID
                from orion.customer
                where Customer_Type_ID =
                   (select Customer_Type_ID
                       from orion.customer_type
                       where Customer_Type =
                       'Orion Club members low activity'))
   group by Customer_ID;
quit;
title;
```

21   s105d03

5.03 Multiple Choice Poll – Correct Answer

What happens when you change the comparison operator to an equal sign?

a. Nothing special, the program runs fine.

b. You get multiple rows returned in your output.

(c.) You get an error message.

d. a and b

```
ERROR: Subquery evaluated to more than one row.
```

31

5.04 Poll – Correct Answer

Can this SELECT statement be used as a subquery?

 Yes

◉ No

A subquery must return values from a single column.

48

5.05 Poll – Correct Answer

The first SELECT statement uses an in-line view to create data that is referenced with the alias **job**. Can **job** also be referenced in the second SELECT statement?

 Yes

◉ No

An in-line view can be referenced only in the SELECT statement where it is defined.

54

5.06 Multiple Choice Poll – Correct Answer

To join the **employee_organization** table with the Step 1 query results, you use the query from Step 1 as which of the following?

   a. an in-line view
   b. a noncorrelated subquery
   c. either a or b
   d. neither a or b

64

5.07 Poll – Correct Answer

Is it possible to use the entire query in Step 2 as a subquery?

◉ Yes
○ No

A subquery can return values for multiple rows, but must return values for only one column. When submitted on its own, the query in Step 2 returns one row and one column, so it can be used as a noncorrelated subquery.

70

Chapter 6   Set Operators

6.1 Introduction to Set Operators

Objectives

- Describe the business scenarios.
- Explore the example data.
- Describe the SQL set operators.

3

Business Scenario

Your manager has requested reports that answer questions, including the following:

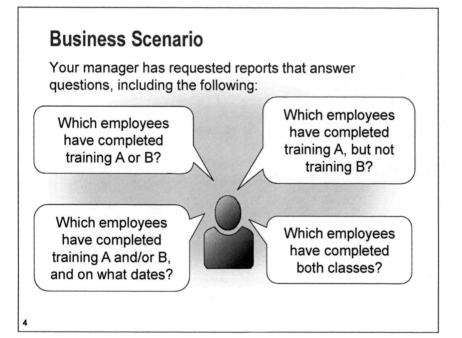

Which employees have completed training A or B?

Which employees have completed training A, but not training B?

Which employees have completed training A and/or B, and on what dates?

Which employees have completed both classes?

4

Business Data

The data required to answer the questions is stored in two tables.

Partial **train_a**

ID	Name	End_Date
11	Bob	15JUN2012
16	Sam	5JUN2012
14	Pete	21JUN2012

Training class A is completed in a single session. End_Date represents the date of training.

Partial **train_b**

Name	ID	SDate	EDate
Bob	11	9JUL2012	13JUL2012
Pam	15	25JUL2012	27JUL2012
Kyle	19	12JUL2012	20JUL2012
Chris	21	29JUL2012	.

Training class B is a multi-session class. SDate is recorded on the first training day. EDate is recorded when the course is complete.

5

Discussion

Can you answer any of the four questions by querying only one table?

1	Which employees have completed training A or B?
2	Which employees have completed training A and/or B, and on what dates?
3	Which employees have completed training A, but not training B?
4	Which employees have completed both classes?

Partial **train_a**

ID	Name	End_Date
11	Bob	15JUN2012
16	Sam	5JUN2012
14	Pete	21JUN2012

Partial **train_b**

Name	ID	SDate	EDate
Bob	11	9JUL2012	13JUL2012
Pam	15	25JUL2012	27JUL2012
Kyle	19	12JUL2012	20JUL2012
Chris	21	29JUL2012	.

6

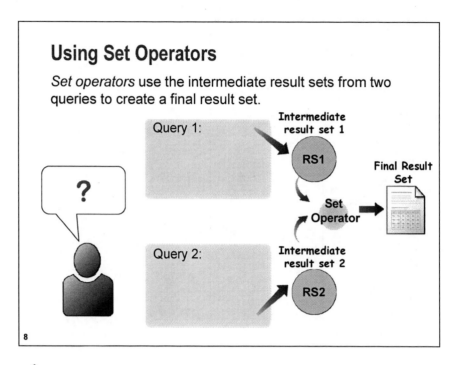

✎ The set operator operates on the result sets produced by the table queries (select queries), not on the actual tables themselves.

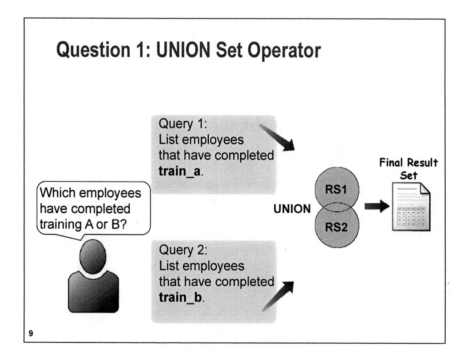

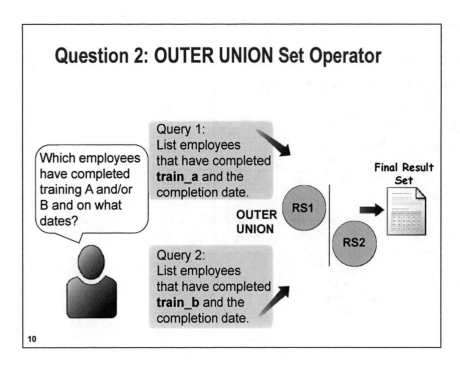

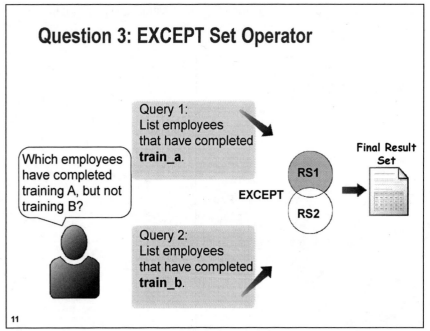

Question 4: INTERSECT Set Operator

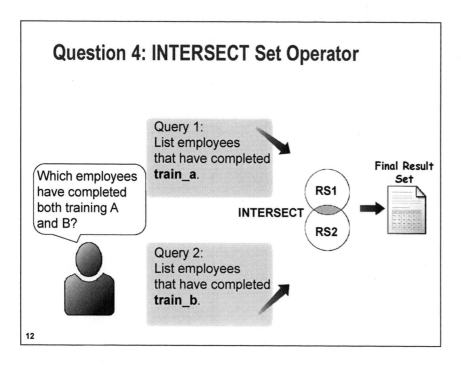

12

Default Behavior of Set Operators

Set Operator	Rows	Columns
UNION	Unique rows from both result sets	Aligned by column position in both result sets
OUTER UNION	All rows from both result sets	All columns from both result sets
EXCEPT	Unique rows from the first result set, that are not in the second result set	Aligned by column position in both result sets
INTERSECT	Unique rows from the first result set that are in the second result set	Aligned by column position in both result sets

13

Using Set Operators

```
SELECT ...
UNION | OUTER UNION | EXCEPT | INTERSECT
<ALL><CORR>
SELECT ...;
```

The modifiers ALL and CORR change the default behavior of the set operators.

ALL modifies the default behavior for rows.
CORR modifies the default behavior for columns.

14

6.01 Poll

By default, the UNION, INTERSECT, and EXCEPT set operators remove duplicate rows from the query output.

○ True
○ False

15

6.2 The UNION Operator

Objectives

- Describe the SQL process when you use the UNION set operator.
- Use the UNION set operator.
- Use the modifiers ALL and CORR.

19

Business Scenario: Question 1

The Education manager needs to know which employees have completed training class A or B.

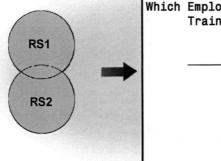

```
Which Employees Have Completed
       Training A or B?

         ID   Name
        _____

         11   Bob
         12   Sue
         14   Pete
         15   Pam
         16   Sam
              . . .
```

20

UNION Operator

The manager requested a report that shows employees from both result sets; the UNION operator is appropriate.

```
title 'Which Employees Have Completed';
title2 'Training A or B?';
proc sql;
select ID, Name from work.train_a
union
select ID, Name from work.train_b
   where EDate is not missing;
quit;
```

```
SELECT ...
UNION <ALL><CORR>
SELECT ...;
```

21

s106d01

Default Behavior of the UNION Operator

Rows

- Rows from both intermediate result sets are concatenated.
- Duplicate rows are removed from the final result set.

Columns

- Columns are matched by position in the select clauses and must be the same data type.
- Column names in the final result set are determined by the first result set.

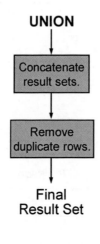

UNION

Concatenate result sets.

Remove duplicate rows.

Final Result Set

22

If the two Intermediate result sets have a different number of columns, then SAS will extend one table with null columns so the two intermediate result sets will have the same number of columns. If Result Set 1 is extended with null columns, then the name of the column in Result Set 2 will be used in the final results.

Viewing the Intermediate Result Sets

UNION

Intermediate Result Set 1	
ID	Name
11	Bob
16	Sam
14	Pete
21	Chris
18	Kim
17	Pat
20	Mary
12	Sue
87	Ted
91	Rand

Intermediate Result Set 2	
ID	Name
11	Bob
15	Pam
19	Kyle
87	Ted

Concatenated Result Set	
ID	Name
11	Bob
16	Sam
14	Pete
21	Chris
18	Kim
17	Pat
20	Mary
12	Sue
87	Ted
91	Rand
11	Bob
15	Pam
19	Kyle
87	Ted

23

Removing Duplicates

UNION

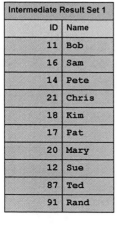

Intermediate Result Set 1	
ID	Name
11	Bob
16	Sam
14	Pete
21	Chris
18	Kim
17	Pat
20	Mary
12	Sue
87	Ted
91	Rand

Intermediate Result Set 2	
ID	Name
11	Bob
15	Pam
19	Kyle
87	Ted

Concatenated Result Set	
ID	Name
11	Bob
16	Sam
14	Pete
21	Chris
18	Kim
17	Pat
20	Mary
12	Sue
87	Ted
91	Rand
~~11~~	~~Bob~~
15	Pam
19	Kyle
~~87~~	~~Ted~~

24

Viewing the Output

PROC SQL Output

```
Which Employees Have Completed
        Training A or B?

            ID  Name
          ───────────────
            11  Bob
            12  Sue
            14  Pete
            15  Pam
            16  Sam
            17  Pat
            18  Kim
            19  Kyle
            20  Mary
            21  Chris
            87  Ted
            91  Rand
```

25

Issues with Default Behavior

Use the * operator to specify that all columns from **train_a** and **train_b** will be used in the intermediate result tables.

```
title 'Union with Defaults';
proc sql;
select * from work.train_a
union
select * from work.train_b
   where EDate is not missing;
quit;
```

s106d02

26

Viewing the Intermediate Result Sets

Intermediate Result Set 1		
ID	Name	Completion Date
11	Bob	15JUN2012
16	Sam	05JUN2012
14	Pete	21JUN2012
21	Chris	07JUN2012
18	Kim	04JUN2012
17	Pat	22JUN2012
20	Mary	11JUN2012
12	Sue	06JUN2012
87	Ted	05JUN2012
91	Rand	07JUN2012

Intermediate Result Set 2			
Name	ID	Start Date	End Date
Bob	11	09JUL2012	13JUL2012
Pam	15	25JUL2012	27JUL2012
Kyle	19	12JUL2012	20JUL2012
Ted	87	09JUL2012	13JUL2012

Align columns by position in the intermediate result sets. Column 1 from result set 1 is aligned with column 1 from result set 2, and so on. Will this work?

27

Viewing the Log

```
title 'UNION with Defaults';
proc sql;
select * from work.train_a
union
select * from work.train_b
    where EDate is not missing;
WARNING: A table has been extended with null columns to perform
the UNION set operation.
ERROR: Column 1 from the first contributor of UNION is not the
same type as its counterpart from the second.
ERROR: Column 2 from the first contributor of UNION is not the
same type as its counterpart from the second.
367  quit;
```

28

s106d02

Behavior of UNION Operator with Modifiers

Rows with ALL modifier

- Rows from both intermediate result sets are concatenated.
- Duplicate rows are *not* removed from the final result tables.

Columns with CORR modifier

- Columns are matched by name and non-matching columns are removed from the intermediate result sets.

29

Use the ALL keyword when either of the following conditions occurs:

- The presence of duplicates in the final result set will not cause problems.
- Duplicates are not possible. For example, there is a unique or primary key constraint on the column.

Issues with Default Behavior: Corrected

Use the CORR modifier to match columns in the intermediate result sets by name.

```
title 'UNION with CORR Modifier';
proc sql;
select * from work.train_a
union corr
select * from work.train_b
   where EDate is not missing;
quit;
```

Result Set 1   Result Set 2

ID ———————————→ Name

Name ——————————→ ID

~~Date~~   ~~SDate~~

                    ~~EDate~~

30   s106d02

Viewing the Output

PROC SQL Output

```
UNION with CORR Modifier

      ID  Name
     ──────────────
      11  Bob
      12  Sue
      14  Pete
      15  Pam
      16  Sam
      17  Pat
      18  Kim
      19  Kyle
      20  Mary
      21  Chris
      87  Ted
      91  Rand
```

31

Setup for the Quiz

Open the program **s106a01**, submit the program, and view the report.

Return to the program, add the ALL keyword with the UNION operator, resubmit the program, and view the report. Answer the following question.

Is there any difference in the output with the ALL keyword? Why?

32

6.02 Quiz

Is there any difference in the output with the ALL keyword? Why?

33

Flow Diagram: UNION Operator

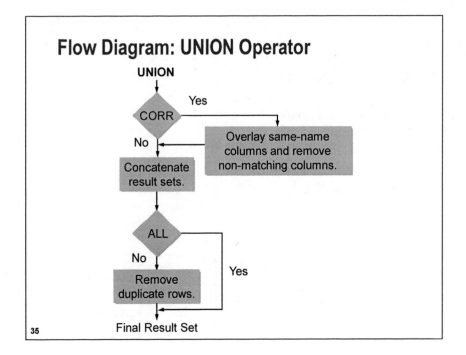

35   Final Result Set

Business Scenario

The management team requested a payroll report for Level I, II, and III Orion Star employees.

RS1

RS2

Payroll Report for Level I, II, and III Employees	
Total Paid to ALL Level I Staff	1,234,567
Total Paid to ALL Level II Staff	1,456,789
Total Paid to ALL Level III Staff	2,123,456

36

Business Data

- The **orion.staff** table contains the **job_title** and **salary** information for all Orion Star employees.
- Submit a separate query for each of the three job title levels.
- Use the UNION set operator twice to combine the intermediate result sets into a single query expression.

Payroll Report for Level I, II, and III Employees	
Total Paid to ALL Level I Staff	1,234,567
Total Paid to ALL Level II Staff	1,456,789
Total Paid to ALL Level III Staff	2,123,456

37

UNION Operator

```
title 'Payroll Report for Level I, II,';
title2 'and III Employees';
proc sql;
select 'Total Paid to ALL Level I Staff',
       sum(Salary) format=comma12.
   from orion.staff
   where scan(Job_Title,-1,' ')='I'
union
select 'Total Paid to ALL Level II Staff',
       sum(Salary) format=comma12.
   from orion.staff
   where scan(Job_Title,-1,' ')='II'
union
select 'Total Paid to ALL Level III Staff',
       sum(Salary) format=comma12.
   from orion.staff
   where scan(Job_Title,-1,' ')='III';
quit;
```

s106d03

38

Viewing the Output

PROC SQL Output

```
          Payroll Report for Level I, II,
                and III Employees

Total Paid to ALL Level I Staff        3,582,630
Total Paid to ALL Level II Staff       3,569,580
Total Paid to ALL Level III Staff      2,296,425
```

39

6.03 Multiple Choice

Is it more or less efficient to use the ALL keyword in a set operation?

○ more efficient
○ less efficient

40

6.3 The OUTER UNION Operator

Objectives

- Describe the SQL process when you use the OUTER UNION set operator and keywords.
- Use the OUTER UNION set operator.
- Compare the SQL OUTER UNION operator to traditional SAS programming.

44

Business Scenario: Question 2

The education manager requested a report that lists which employees have completed training A and/or B, and on what dates?

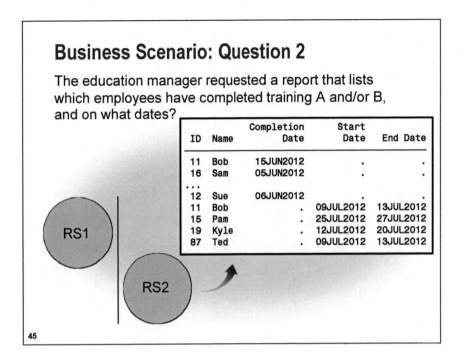

ID	Name	Completion Date	Start Date	End Date
11	Bob	15JUN2012	.	.
16	Sam	05JUN2012	.	.
...				
12	Sue	06JUN2012	.	.
11	Bob	.	09JUL2012	13JUL2012
15	Pam	.	25JUL2012	27JUL2012
19	Kyle	.	12JUL2012	20JUL2012
87	Ted	.	09JUL2012	13JUL2012

45

OUTER UNION Operator

The report needs to keep all rows and all columns from the two intermediate result sets. The OUTER UNION operator will accomplish this.

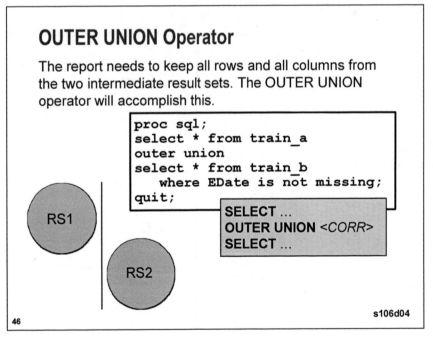

```
proc sql;
select * from train_a
outer union
select * from train_b
    where EDate is not missing;
quit;
```

SELECT ...
OUTER UNION <CORR>
SELECT ...

s106d04

46

Default Behavior of the OUTER UNION Operator

Rows

- Rows from both intermediate result sets are concatenated.
- Duplicate rows are not removed from the final result set.

Columns

- All columns from both result sets are selected. Common columns are not overlaid.

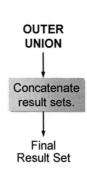

OUTER
UNION

↓

Concatenate
result sets.

↓

Final
Result Set

47

Viewing the Output

PROC SQL Output

ID	Name	Completion Date	Name	ID	Start Date	End Date
11	Bob	15JUN2012		.	.	.
16	Sam	05JUN2012		.	.	.
14	Pete	21JUN2012		.	.	.
21	Chris	07JUN2012		.	.	.
18	Kim	04JUN2012		.	.	.
17	Pat	22JUN2012		.	.	.
20	Mary	11JUN2012		.	.	.
12	Sue	06JUN2012		.	.	.
87	Ted	05JUN2012		.	.	.
91	Rand	07JUN2012		.	.	.
.		.	Bob	11	09JUL2012	13JUL2012
.		.	Pam	15	25JUL2012	27JUL2012
.		.	Kyle	19	12JUL2012	20JUL2012
.		.	Ted	87	09JUL2012	13JUL2012

48

Behavior of OUTER UNION with Modifiers

Columns with CORR modifier

- All columns from both result sets are selected and common columns are overlaid.

✎ The ALL modifier is not applicable with the OUTER UNION operator. This is the default behavior.

49

OUTER UNION Operator

The previous report can be improved by overlaying the common columns. The OUTER UNION operator with the CORR modifier will accomplish this.

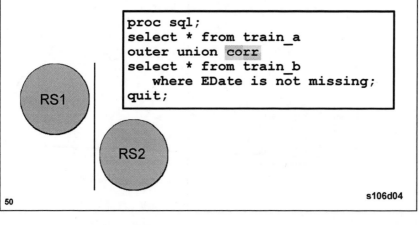

```
proc sql;
select * from train_a
outer union corr
select * from train_b
   where EDate is not missing;
quit;
```

RS1

RS2

50   s106d04

✎ OUTER UNION CORR is useful when you have two or more source tables with some columns in common and extra columns that do not exist in all tables. You can use this technique if you want to include at least one of those extra columns in the output.

Viewing the Output

PROC SQL Output

ID	Name	Completion Date	Start Date	End Date
11	Bob	15JUN2012	.	.
16	Sam	05JUN2012	.	.
14	Pete	21JUN2012	.	.
21	Chris	07JUN2012	.	.
18	Kim	04JUN2012	.	.
17	Pat	22JUN2012	.	.
20	Mary	11JUN2012	.	.
12	Sue	06JUN2012	.	.
87	Ted	05JUN2012	.	.
91	Rand	07JUN2012	.	.
11	Bob	.	09JUL2012	13JUL2012
15	Pam	.	25JUL2012	27JUL2012
19	Kyle	.	12JUL2012	20JUL2012
87	Ted	.	09JUL2012	13JUL2012

51

6.04 Multiple Choice Poll

What DATA step statement yields the same results
as OUTER UNION CORR?

a. MERGE

b. APPEND

c. SET

d. STACK

52

SQL versus Traditional SAS Programming

The following programs produce the same report:

```
data trained;
    set train_a train_b;
run;
proc print data=trained label noobs;
run;
```

```
proc sql;
select * from train_a
outer union corr
select * from train_b;
quit;
```

54   s106d06

Exercises

If you restarted your SAS session since the last exercise, open and submit the **libname.sas** program found in the data folder.

Level 1

1. **Using the UNION Operator**

   Create a report that displays the total salary for female and male sales representatives and the total number of female and male sales representatives. The **orion.salesstaff** table contains information about all the Orion Star sales representatives, including **Salary** and **Gender**. The query should do the following:

   - Create the first row of the report. Use the constant text **Total Paid to All Female Sales Representatives**, **SUM(Salary)**, and the total number of rows using the COUNT(*) function. Summarize data in the **orion.salesstaff** table for those rows that have **Gender** = 'F' and **Job_Title** containing **'Rep'**.

   - Use the appropriate SET operator.

   - Create the second row of the report. Use the constant text **Total Paid to All Male Sales Representatives**, **SUM(Salary)**, and the total number of rows using the COUNT(*) function. Summarize data in the **orion.salesstaff** table for those rows that have **Gender** = 'M' and **Job_Title** containing **'Rep'**.

- Provide a title for the report as shown below.

PROC SQL Output

```
                      Payroll Report for Sales Representatives


                                                                 Total

       Total Paid to All Female Sales Representatives    $1,898,804     68
       Total Paid to All Male Sales Representatives      $2,655,678     95
```

2. Using the OUTER UNION Operator with the CORR Keyword

Create a report that displays the sales data for the first and second quarters of 2011. The **orion.qtr1** table contains the sales data for the first quarter, and the **orion.qtr2** table contains the sales data for the second quarter.

Partial PROC SQL Output

```
                       First and Second Quarter 2011 Sales


                                              Date
                                         Order was      Date
                       Order            placed by   Order was
           Order ID     Type  Customer ID  Customer   Delivered  Employee ID


          1241054779      3          24  02JAN2011  05JAN2011           .
          1241063739      1          89  03JAN2011  04JAN2011           .
                            ...  ...  ...
          1241731828      1          31  18MAR2011  18MAR2011           .
          1241789227      3       17023  25MAR2011  30MAR2011           .
          1241895594      1          56  05APR2011  09APR2011      121051
          1241909303      0       46966  07APR2011  08APR2011    99999999
                            ...  ...  ...
          1242647539      1          45  27JUN2011  27JUN2011      121109
          1242657273      1          90  28JUN2011  28JUN2011      121037
```

Level 2

3. Comparing UNION and OUTER UNION Operators

Stack the **orion.qtr1** and **orion.qtr2** tables to produce a single report.

a. Use the UNION operator to stack the data in **orion.qtr1** and **orion.qtr2**.

b. Use the OUTER UNION operator without the CORR keyword to stack the data in **orion.qtr1** and **orion.qtr2**. Set the LINESIZE system option to 140 to prevent wrapping of the SQL output.

c. Were the final results the same? If not, how did they differ? _____

_____

d. Can the UNION operator and OUTER UNION operator yield the same results if you use the CORR keyword in this example? _____

6.4 The EXCEPT Operator

Objectives

- Describe the SQL process when you use the EXCEPT set operator.
- Use the EXCEPT set operator.
- Use the modifiers ALL and CORR.

58

Business Scenario: Question 3

The education manager requested a report that lists which employees have taken training A, but not training B.

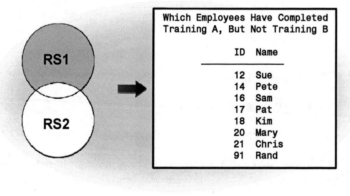

```
Which Employees Have Completed
Training A, But Not Training B

        ID  Name
        ──────────
        12  Sue
        14  Pete
        16  Sam
        17  Pat
        18  Kim
        20  Mary
        21  Chris
        91  Rand
```

59

EXCEPT Operator

This report lists the employees who have completed training A, but not training B. The EXCEPT operator will accomplish this.

```
title 'Which Employees Have Completed';
title2 'Training A, But Not Training B';
proc sql;
select ID, Name from train_a
except
select ID, Name from train_b
   where Edate is not missing;
quit;
```

SELECT ...
EXCEPT *<ALL><CORR>*
SELECT ...

60   s106d07

Default Behavior of the EXCEPT Operator

Rows

- Duplicate rows are removed from the intermediate result sets.
- Rows from the first intermediate result set that are not in the second intermediate result set are selected.

Columns

- Columns are matched by position and must be the same data type.
- Column names in the final result set are determined by the first result set.

61

Viewing the Intermediate Result Sets

EXCEPT

Intermediate Result Set 1	
ID	Name
11	Bob
16	Sam
14	Pete
21	Chris
18	Kim
17	Pat
20	Mary
12	Sue
87	Ted
91	Rand

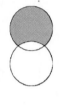

Intermediate Result Set 2	
ID	Name
11	Bob
15	Pam
19	Kyle
87	Ted

62

Removing Duplicate Rows

EXCEPT

Intermediate Result Set 1	
ID	Name
11	Bob
16	Sam
14	Pete
21	Chris
18	Kim
17	Pat
20	Mary
12	Sue
87	Ted
91	Rand

Intermediate Result Set 2	
ID	Name
11	Bob
15	Pam
19	Kyle
87	Ted

63

Removing Matching Rows

EXCEPT

Intermediate Result Set 1	
ID	Name
~~11~~	~~Bob~~
16	Sam
14	Pete
21	Chris
18	Kim
17	Pat
20	Mary
12	Sue
~~07~~	~~Ted~~
91	Rand

Intermediate Result Set 2	
ID	Name
11	Bob
15	Pam
19	Kyle
87	Ted

64

Viewing the Output

PROC SQL Output

```
Which Employees Have Completed
Training A, But Not Training B

    ID   Name
   ─────────────
    12   Sue
    14   Pete
    16   Sam
    17   Pat
    18   Kim
    20   Mary
    21   Chris
    91   Rand
```

65

Copyright © 2013, SAS Institute Inc., Cary, North Carolina, USA. ALL RIGHTS RESERVED.

Behavior of EXCEPT Operator with Modifiers

Rows with the ALL modifier

- Duplicate rows are *not* removed from the intermediate result sets.

- Rows from the first intermediate result set that are not in the second intermediate result set are selected.

Columns with the CORR modifier

- Columns are matched by name and non-matching columns are removed from the intermediate result sets.

66

Using a Set Operator in an In-Line View

The previous query can easily become an in-line view used to determine how many employees that have completed training A have not completed training B.

```
proc sql;
select count(ID) as Count
   from (select ID, Name from train_a
         except
         select ID, Name from train_b
            where Edate is not missing);
quit;
```

PROC SQL Output

Count
8

s106d08

67

Setup for the Poll

View the PROC SQL code below and respond to the
following True/False statement: Adding the CORR
keyword to this code will change the results.

```
proc sql;
select ID, Name from train_a
except
select ID, Name from train_b;
quit;
```

68

6.05 Poll

Adding the CORR keyword to this code will change the
results.

○ True
○ False

69

Flow Diagram: EXCEPT Operator

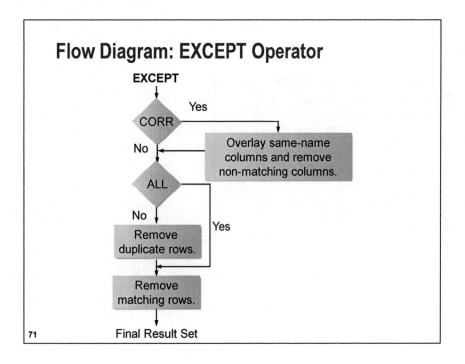

71

6.06 Poll

By default, the EXCEPT set operator selects **all** of the rows from the first result set that are not in the second result set.

O True

O False

72

6.5 The INTERSECT Operator

Objectives

- Describe the SQL process when you use the INTERSECT set operator.
- Use the INTERSECT set operator.
- Use the modifiers ALL and CORR.

76

Business Scenario: Question 4

The education manager has requested a report that lists which employees have completed both training classes.

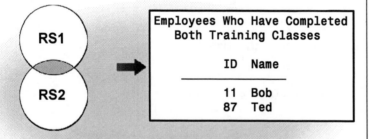

```
Employees Who Have Completed
     Both Training Classes

            ID   Name
            _____
            11   Bob
            87   Ted
```

77

INTERSECT Operator

This report requires rows that exist in both **train_a** and **train_b**. The INTERSECT operator will accomplish this.

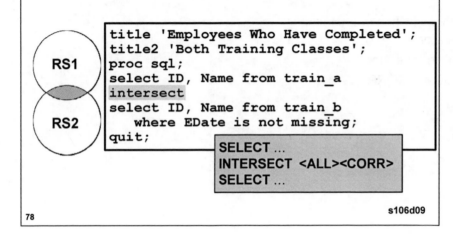

```
title 'Employees Who Have Completed';
title2 'Both Training Classes';
proc sql;
select ID, Name from train_a
intersect
select ID, Name from train_b
   where EDate is not missing;
quit;
```

SELECT ...
INTERSECT <ALL><CORR>
SELECT ...

s106d09

78

Default Behavior of the INTERSECT Operator

Rows

- Duplicate rows are removed from the intermediate result sets.

- Rows from the first intermediate result set that are also in the second intermediate result set are selected.

Columns

- Columns are matched by position and must be the same data type.

- Column names in the final result set are determined by the first result set.

79

Viewing the Intermediate Result Sets

INTERSECT

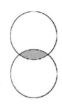

Intermediate Result Set 1	
ID	Name
11	Bob
16	Sam
14	Pete
21	Chris
18	Kim
17	Pat
20	Mary
12	Sue
87	Ted
91	Rand

Intermediate Result Set 2	
ID	Name
11	Bob
15	Pam
19	Kyle
87	Ted

80

Removing Duplicate Rows

INTERSECT

Intermediate Result Set 1	
ID	Name
11	Bob
16	Sam
14	Pete
21	Chris
18	Kim
17	Pat
20	Mary
12	Sue
87	Ted
91	Rand

Intermediate Result Set 2	
ID	Name
11	Bob
15	Pam
19	Kyle
87	Ted

81

Removing Non-Matching Rows

INTERSECT

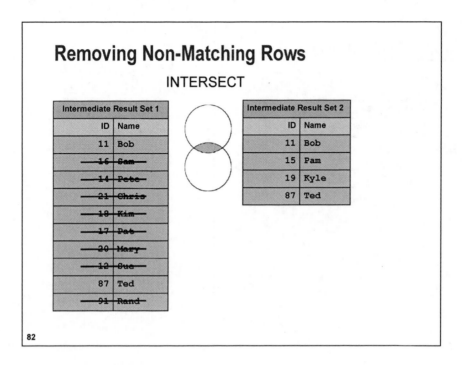

Intermediate Result Set 1	
ID	Name
11	Bob
~~16~~	~~Sam~~
~~14~~	~~Pete~~
~~21~~	~~Chris~~
~~18~~	~~Kim~~
~~17~~	~~Pat~~
~~20~~	~~Mary~~
~~12~~	~~Sue~~
87	Ted
~~91~~	~~Rand~~

Intermediate Result Set 2	
ID	Name
11	Bob
15	Pam
19	Kyle
87	Ted

82

Viewing the Output

PROC SQL Output

```
Employees Who Have Completed
    Both Training Classes

        ID   Name
        ─────────────
        11   Bob
        87   Ted
```

83

Behavior of the INTERSECT Operator with Modifiers

Rows with the ALL modifier

- Duplicate rows are **not** removed from the intermediate result sets.

- Rows from the first intermediate result set that are also in the second intermediate result set are selected.

Columns with the CORR modifier

- Columns are matched by name and non-matching columns are removed from the intermediate result sets.

84

Flow Diagram: INTERSECT Operator

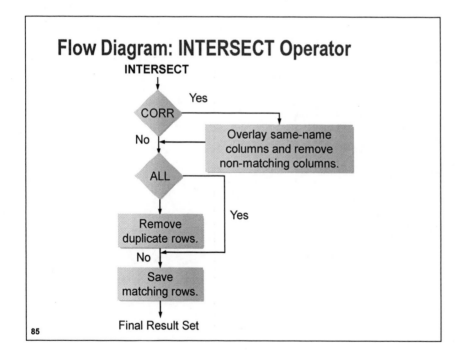

85

Business Scenario

Bob, a team manager, requests your help. He wants to know if there were any of his team members who had not started either training class. He provided you with a table of his team members.

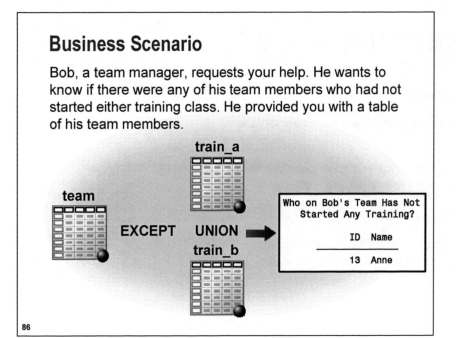

86

Combining Set Operators

This report needs to return any rows in the **team** table that are not in either **train_a** or **train_b**.

```
title "Who on Bob's Team Has Not";
title2 'Started Any Training';
proc sql;
select ID, Name from team
except
(select ID, Name from train_a
 union
 select ID, Name from train_b);
quit;
```

s106d10

87

✎   Set operators follow this order of precedence unless they are overridden by parentheses in the expressions: INTERSECT is evaluated first. OUTER UNION, UNION, and EXCEPT have the same level of precedence.

Viewing the UNION Result Set

The UNION operator will return an intermediate result set of all employees that have started either training class.

Intermediate Result Set UNION

ID	Name
11	Bob
12	Sue
14	Pete
15	Pam
16	Sam
17	Pat
18	Kim
19	Kyle
20	Mary
21	Chris
87	Ted
91	Rand

88

Removing the Duplicates

EXCEPT

Intermediate Result Bob's Team

ID	Name
11	Bob
~~11~~	~~Bob~~
12	Sue
13	Anne
14	Pete
15	Pam
16	Sam
17	Pat
18	Kim
19	Kyle
20	Mary
21	Chris

Intermediate Result Set UNION

ID	Name
11	Bob
12	Sue
14	Pete
15	Pam
16	Sam
17	Pat
18	Kim
19	Kyle
20	Mary
21	Chris
87	Ted
91	Rand

89

Removing the Matching Rows

Intermediate Result Bob's Team	
ID	Name
~~11~~	~~Bob~~
~~11~~	~~Bob~~
~~12~~	~~Sue~~
13	Anne
~~14~~	~~Pete~~
~~15~~	~~Pam~~
~~16~~	~~Sam~~
~~17~~	~~Pat~~
~~18~~	~~Kim~~
~~19~~	~~Kyle~~
~~20~~	~~Mary~~
~~21~~	~~Chris~~

EXCEPT

Intermediate Result Set UNION	
ID	Name
11	Bob
12	Sue
14	Pete
15	Pam
16	Sam
17	Pat
18	Kim
19	Kyle
20	Mary
21	Chris
87	Ted
91	Rand

90

Viewing the Output

PROC SQL Output

Who on Bob's Team Has Not Started Any Training?	
ID	Name
13	Anne

91

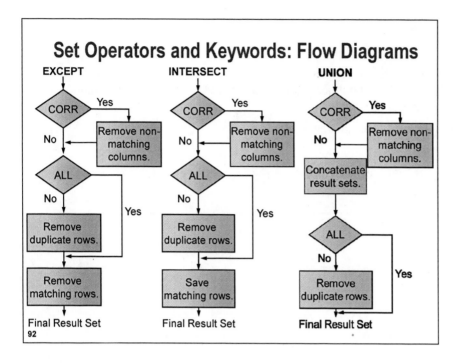

Set Operators and Keywords: Flow Diagrams

Exercises

If you restarted your SAS session since the last exercise, open and submit the **libname.sas** program found in the data folder.

Level 1

4. Using the EXCEPT Operator

Create a report that displays the employee identification numbers of employees who have phone numbers, but do not appear to have address information. The **orion.employee_phones** table contains **Employee_ID** and **Phone_Number**. If an employee's address is on file, the **orion.employee_addresses** table contains the **Employee_ID** value and address information. The query should

- use the column **Employee_ID** from **orion.employee_phones**
- use the appropriate SET operator
- use the column **Employee_ ID** from **orion.employee_addresses**.

PROC SQL Output

Employee IDs with Phone Numbers But Not Address Information
Employee_ID
12099
20683
21149

5. Using the INTERSECT Operator

Create a report that shows **Customer_ID** for all customers who placed orders. The **orion.order_fact** table contains information about the orders that were placed by Orion Star customers, including **Customer_ID**. The **orion.customer** table contains information about all Orion Star customers, including **Customer_ID**. The query should

- use the column **Customer_ID** from **orion.order_fact**
- use the appropriate SET operator
- use the column **Customer_ ID** from **orion.customer**.

Partial PROC SQL Output

```
                    Customers Who Placed Orders

                            Customer ID
                            _____

                                      4
                                      5
                                      9
                          ... ... ...
```

Level 2

6. Using the EXCEPT Operator to Count Rows

Create a report that displays the total count of employees who did not make any charitable donations. The **orion.employee_organization** table contains a record for every employee in the Orion Star organization and includes the employee identification numbers. The **orion.employee_donations** table contains records only for employees who made charitable donations, including the **Employee_ID** value.

PROC SQL Output

```
                                  No.
                               Employees
                                 w/ No
                               Charitable
                               Donations
                               _____

                                  300
```

7. Using the INTERSECT Operator to Count Rows

Create a report that shows the total number of customers who placed orders. The **orion.order_fact** table contains information about the orders that were placed by Orion Star customers, including **Customer_ID**. The **orion.customer** table contains information about all Orion Star customers, including **Customer_ID**.

PROC SQL Output

```
                                  No.
                               Customers
                               w/ Orders
                               _____

                                   75
```

Challenge

8. Using the EXCEPT Operator with a Subquery

Create a report that displays the employee identification numbers and names of sales representatives who did not sell any products in 2011. The **orion.sales** table contains the **Employee_ID** values of all sales representatives. The **orion.order_fact** table contains the **Employee_ID** value of the salesperson and other information about all sales that were made. The **orion.employee_addresses** table contains the **Employee_ID** and **Employee_Name** values of all Orion Star employees. Provide a title for the report as indicated in the sample output, and include the row number as part of the report.

Partial PROC SQL Output

```
               Sales Reps Who Made No Sales in 2011

          Row   Employee_ID  Employee_Name

           1        121044   Abbott, Ray
           2        120145   Aisbitt, Sandy
           3        121038   Anstey, David
           4        121030   Areu, Jeryl
           5        121062   Armant, Debra
           6        120144   Barbis, Viney
           7        120168   Barcoe, Selina
                    ... ... ...
```

9. Using the INTERSECT Operator with a Subquery

Create a report that includes **Customer_ID** and **Customer_Name** for all customers who placed orders. The **orion.order_fact** table contains information about the orders that were placed by Orion Star customers, including **Customer_ID**. The **orion.customer** table contains information about all Orion Star customers, including **Customer_ID** and **Customer_Name**.

Partial PROC SQL Output

```
               Name of Customers Who Placed Orders

          Customer ID  Customer Name

                    4   James Kvarniq
                    5   Sandrina Stephano
                    9   Cornelia Krahl
                   10   Karen Ballinger
                   11   Elke Wallstab
                   12   David Black
                   13   Markus Sepke
                   16   Ulrich Heyde
                   17   Jimmie Evans
                   18   Tonie Asmussen
                   19   Oliver S. Füßling
                   20   Michael Dineley
                   23   Tulio Devereaux
                   24   Robyn Klem
                    ... ... ...
```

6.6 Solutions

Solutions to Exercises

1. **Using the UNION Operator**

```
*** s106s01 ***;

proc sql;
title 'Payroll Report for Sales Representatives';
select 'Total Paid to All Female Sales Representatives',
       sum(Salary) format=dollar14., count(*) label='Total'
   from orion.salesstaff
   where gender='F' and  Job_Title like '%Rep%'
union
select 'Total Paid to All Male Sales Representatives',
       sum(Salary) format=dollar14., count(*) label='Total'
   from orion.salesstaff
   where gender='M' and Job_Title like '%Rep%';
quit;
title;
```

2. **Using the OUTER UNION Operator with the CORR Keyword**

```
*** s106s02 ***;

proc sql;
title 'First and Second Quarter 2011 Sales ';
select *
   from orion.qtr1
outer union corr
select *
   from orion.qtr2;
quit;
title;
```

3. **Comparing UNION and OUTER UNION Operators**

   a. The **Customer_ID** column contains some **Employee_ID** values because the columns are overlaid.

```
*** s106s03 ***;

  /* a */
proc sql;
title 'Results with UNION operator';
select *
   from orion.qtr1
union
select *
   from orion.qtr2;
quit;
title;
```

Partial PROC SQL Output

```
                          Results with UNION operator

                                      Date
                                 Order was       Date        Date
                       Order     placed by   Order was   Order was
        Order ID        Type   Customer ID    Customer   Delivered   Delivered
        ────────────────────────────────────────────────────────────────────────
               .           1        120127   20JUN1960   13MAY2011   13MAY2011
               .           3      99999999   14NOV2151   11MAY2011   14MAY2011
        1241054779         3            24   02JAN2011   05JAN2011           .
        1241063739         1            89   03JAN2011   04JAN2011           .
        1241066216         1           171   04JAN2011   04JAN2011           .
        ...
        1241686210         1            10   13MAR2011   19MAR2011           .
        1241715610         1            92   16MAR2011   16MAR2011           .
        1241731828         1            31   18MAR2011   18MAR2011           .
        1241789227         3         17023   25MAR2011   30MAR2011           .
        1241895594         1        121051   26FEB1960   05APR2011   09APR2011
        1241909303         0      99999999   02AUG2088   07APR2011   08APR2011
        1241930625         3      99999999   28JAN1960   09APR2011   14APR2011
        1241977403         1        120152   20JUN1960   15APR2011   15APR2011
```

b. With the OUTER UNION operator, all rows from both tables are selected. This includes both unique and non-unique rows. The columns are not overlaid. Examine the column for **Employee_ID**.

```
/* b */
options ls=140;
proc sql;
title 'Results with OUTER UNION operator';
select *
   from orion.qtr1
outer union
select *
   from orion.qtr2;
quit;
title;
```

Partial PROC SQL Output

```
                                                          Results with OUTER UNION operator

                              Date                                                                    Date
                         Order was       Date                                                    Order was       Date
               Order     placed by   Order was               Order                               placed by   Order was
    Order ID    Type   Customer ID    Customer   Delivered    Order ID   Type  Employee ID  Customer ID   Customer   Delivered
    ──────────────────────────────────────────────────────────────────────────────────────────────────────────────────────────
    1241054779    3           24   02JAN2011   05JAN2011         .        .        .            .           .           .
    1241063739    1           89   03JAN2011   04JAN2011         .        .        .            .           .           .
    1241066216    1          171   04JAN2011   04JAN2011         .        .        .            .           .           .
    1241086052    3           53   06JAN2011   09JAN2011         .        .        .            .           .           .
    1241147641    1           53   13JAN2011   13JAN2011         .        .        .            .           .           .
    1241235281    1          171   23JAN2011   30JAN2011         .        .        .            .           .           .
    1241244297    1          111   24JAN2011   24JAN2011         .        .        .            .           .           .
    1241263172    3         3959   25JAN2011   26JAN2011         .        .        .            .           .           .
    1241286432    3           27   28JAN2011   02FEB2011         .        .        .            .           .           .
    1241298131    2         2806   29JAN2011   08FEB2011         .        .        .            .           .           .
    1241359997    1           12   05FEB2011   05FEB2011         .        .        .            .           .           .
    1241371145    1          171   07FEB2011   07FEB2011         .        .        .            .           .           .
    1241390440    1           41   09FEB2011   09FEB2011         .        .        .            .           .           .
    1241461856    1           18   16FEB2011   17FEB2011         .        .        .            .           .           .
    1241561055    1          171   28FEB2011   28FEB2011         .        .        .            .           .           .
```

1241623505	3	24	06MAR2011	09MAR2011	.	.	.	.	.	.
1241645664	2	70100	09MAR2011	13MAR2011	.	.	.	.	.	.
1241652707	3	27	09MAR2011	14MAR2011	.	.	.	.	.	.
1241686210	1	10	13MAR2011	19MAR2011	.	.	.	.	.	.
1241715610	1	92	16MAR2011	16MAR2011	.	.	.	.	.	.
1241731828	1	31	18MAR2011	18MAR2011	.	.	.	.	.	.
1241789227	3	17023	25MAR2011	30MAR2011	.	.	.	.	.	.
.	.	.	.	.	1241895594	1	121051	56	05APR2011	09APR2011
.	.	.	.	.	1241909303	0	99999999	46966	07APR2011	08APR2011
.	.	.	.	.	1241930625	3	99999999	27	09APR2011	14APR2011
.	.	.	.	.	1241977403	1	120152	171	15APR2011	15APR2011
.	.	.	.	.	1242012259	1	121040	10	18APR2011	12APR2011
.	.	.	.	.	1242012269	1	121040	45	18APR2011	18APR2011
.	.	.	.	.	1242035131	1	120132	183	21APR2011	21APR2011
.	.	.	.	.	1242076538	3	99999999	31	25APR2011	29APR2011
.	.	.	.	.	1242130888	1	121086	92	01MAY2011	01MAY2011
.	.	.	.	.	1242140006	4	99999999	5	02MAY2011	07MAY2011
.	.	.	.	.	1242140009	2	99999999	90	02MAY2011	04MAY2011
.	.	.	.	.	1242149082	1	121032	90	03MAY2011	03MAY2011
.	.	.	.	.	1242159212	3	99999999	5	04MAY2011	09MAY2011
.	.	.	.	.	1242161468	3	99999999	2550	04MAY2011	09MAY2011
.	.	.	.	.	1242162201	3	99999999	46966	05MAY2011	06MAY2011
.	.	.	.	.	1242173926	3	99999999	1033	06MAY2011	10MAY2011
.	.	.	.	.	1242185055	1	120136	41	08MAY2011	08MAY2011
.	.	.	.	.	.	3	99999999	70079	11MAY2011	14MAY2011
.	.	.	.	.	.	1	120127	171	13MAY2011	13MAY2011
.	.	.	.	.	1242259863	2	99999999	70187	16MAY2011	21MAY2011
.	.	.	.	.	1242265757	1	121105	10	16MAY2011	16MAY2011
.	.	.	.	.	1242449327	3	99999999	27	26JUL2011	26JUL2011
.	.	.	.	.	1242458099	1	121071	10	06JUN2011	06JUN2011
.	.	.	.	.	1242467585	3	99999999	34	07JUN2011	13JUN2011
.	.	.	.	.	1242477751	3	99999999	31	08JUN2011	12JUN2011
.	.	.	.	.	1242493791	1	121056	5	10JUN2011	10JUN2011
.	.	.	.	.	1242502670	1	121067	31	11JUN2011	11JUN2011
.	.	.	.	.	1242515373	3	99999999	17023	13JUN2011	18JUN2011
.	.	.	.	.	1242534503	3	99999999	70165	15JUN2011	22JUN2011
.	.	.	.	.	1242557584	2	99999999	89	17JUN2011	21JUN2011
.	.	.	.	.	1242559569	1	120130	171	18JUN2011	18JUN2011

c. Were the final results the same? If not, how did they differ? **No, the final results are different. When the UNION operator is used, the Customer_ID column contains some Employee_ID values because the columns are overlaid. When the OUTER UNION operator is used, all of the rows from both tables are selected. These rows include both unique and non-unique rows. Also, notice that there is a separate column for Employee_ID, because the columns are not overlaid when you use the OUTER UNION operator.**

d. Can the UNION operator and OUTER UNION operator yield the same results if you use the CORR keyword in this example? **No, the UNION operator with the CORR keyword cannot yield the same results as the OUTER UNION operator with the CORR keyword for this example. This is because UNION CORR discards columns that do not have matching names whereas OUTER UNION CORR retains all columns.**

```
/* d - NO*/
proc sql;
title 'Results with UNION operator and CORR modifier';
select *
   from orion.qtr1
union corr
select *
   from orion.qtr2;
quit;
title;
```

```
proc sql;
title 'Results with OUTER UNION operator and CORR modifier';
select *
   from orion.qtr1
outer union corr
select *
   from orion.qtr2;
quit;
title;
```

4. Using the EXCEPT Operator

```
*** s106s04 ***;

proc sql;
title "Employee IDs with Phone Numbers But Not Address Information";
select Employee_ID
   from orion.employee_phones
except
select Employee_ID
   from orion.employee_addresses;
quit;
title;


   /* Alternative Solution using the CORR keyword */
proc sql;
title "Employee IDs with Phone Numbers But Not Address Information";
select *
   from orion.employee_phones
except corr
select *
   from orion.employee_addresses;
quit;
title;
```

5. Using the INTERSECT Operator

```
*** s106s05 ***;

proc sql;
title 'Customers Who Placed Orders';
select Customer_ID
   from orion.order_fact
intersect
select Customer_ID
   from orion.customer;
quit;
title;
```

6. Using the EXCEPT Operator to Count Rows

```
*** s106s06 ***;

proc sql;
```

```
select count(*) label='No. Employees w/ No Charitable Donations'
   from (select Employee_ID
              from orion.employee_organization
          except
          select Employee_ID
              from orion.employee_donations);
quit;
```

7. Using the INTERSECT Operator to Count Rows

```
*** s106s07 ***;

proc sql;
select count(*) label='No. Customers w/ Orders'
   from (select Customer_ID
              from orion.order_fact
          intersect
          select Customer_ID
              from orion.customer);
quit;
title;
```

8. Using the EXCEPT Operator with a Subquery

```
*** s106s08 ***;

proc sql number;
title 'Sales Reps Who Made No Sales in 2011';
select Employee_ID, Employee_Name
   from orion.employee_addresses
   where Employee_ID in
       (select Employee_ID
           from orion.sales
           where Job_Title like '%Rep%'
        except all
        select Employee_ID
           from orion.order_fact
           where year(Order_Date)=2011);
quit;
title;
```

9. Using the INTERSECT Operator with a Subquery

```
*** s106s09 ***;

proc sql;
title 'Name of Customers Who Placed Orders';
select Customer_ID, Customer_Name
   from orion.customer
   where Customer_ID in
       (select Customer_ID
           from orion.order_fact
        intersect
        select Customer_ID
```

```
        from orion.customer);
quit;
title;
```

Solutions to Student Activities (Polls/Quizzes)

6.01 Poll – Correct Answer

By default, the UNION, INTERSECT, and EXCEPT set operators remove duplicate rows from the query output.

- ⦿ True
- ○ False

16

6.02 Quiz – Correct Answer

Is there any difference in the output with the ALL keyword? Why?

Yes, Bob and Ted are included twice. This is because they have completed both training classes. Without the ALL keyword, duplicates are removed.

34

6.03 Multiple Choice – Correct Answer

Is it more or less efficient to use the ALL keyword in a set operation?

- ⦿ more efficient
- ○ less efficient

A second pass of the data is not is required to determine whether duplicates exist.

41

6.04 Multiple Choice Poll – Correct Answer

What DATA step statement yields the same results as OUTER UNION CORR?

- a. MERGE
- b. APPEND
- ⓒ. SET
- d. STACK

53

6.05 Poll – Correct Answer

Adding the CORR keyword to this code will change the result.

○ True
◉ False

The columns in the two intermediate result sets are determined by the individual queries. They are the same in both intermediate result sets, so the CORR modifier will not change the result.

70

6.06 Poll – Correct Answer

By default, the EXCEPT set operator selects *all* of the rows from the first result set that are not in the second result set.

○ True
◉ False

By default, the EXCEPT operator eliminates duplicate rows first. It selects only *unique* rows from the first result set that are not in the second result set.

73

Chapter 7   Creating Tables and Views

7.1 Creating Tables with the SQL Procedure

Objectives

- Create a new table and add data using a single query.
- Create a new empty table by copying column structure from an existing table.
- Create a new empty table by defining the column structure.
- Add data into a table.

3

Creating a New Table

There are three ways to create new tables in PROC SQL.

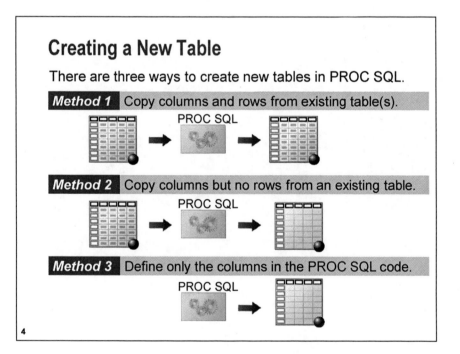

Method 1 Copy columns and rows from existing table(s).

PROC SQL

Method 2 Copy columns but no rows from an existing table.

PROC SQL

Method 3 Define only the columns in the PROC SQL code.

PROC SQL

4

Business Scenario: Method 1

Management wants to recognize employee birthdays. You need to write code to generate a table with each employee's birth month. Existing tables contain the columns and rows that you need.

5

Business Data

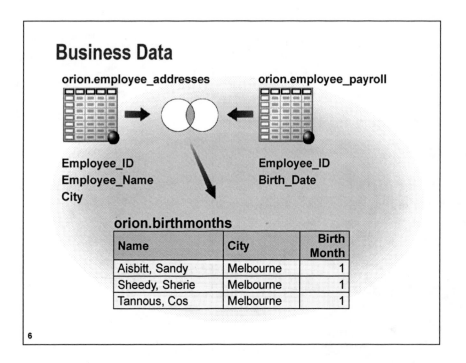

orion.employee_addresses

Employee_ID
Employee_Name
City

orion.employee_payroll

Employee_ID
Birth_Date

orion.birthmonths

Name	City	Birth Month
Aisbitt, Sandy	Melbourne	1
Sheedy, Sherie	Melbourne	1
Tannous, Cos	Melbourne	1

6

Creating a Table: Method 1

For this task, use method 1. Create a table that contains
columns and rows returned by a query on existing tables.

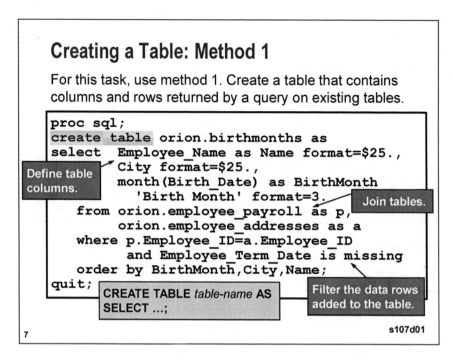

```
proc sql;
create table orion.birthmonths as
select  Employee_Name as Name format=$25.,
        City format=$25.,
        month(Birth_Date) as BirthMonth
          'Birth Month' format=3.
    from orion.employee_payroll as p,
         orion.employee_addresses as a
    where p.Employee_ID=a.Employee_ID
        and Employee_Term_Date is missing
    order by BirthMonth,City,Name;
quit;
```

Define table columns.

Join tables.

CREATE TABLE *table-name* AS SELECT ...;

Filter the data rows added to the table.

s107d01

7

This method is most often used to create subsets or supersets of tables. This is the only method that
creates and populates a table in one statement.

The CREATE TABLE statement does not produce a report. A separate SELECT statement is required to
produce a report based on the new table.

Viewing the Log

```
proc sql;
create table orion.birthmonths as
select  Employee_Name as Name format=$25.,
        City format=$25.,
        month(Birth_Date) as BirthMonth
          'Birth Month' format=3.
   from orion.employee_payroll as p,
        orion.employee_addresses as a
   where p.Employee_ID=
         a.Employee_ID
         and Employee_Term_Date is missing
   order by BirthMonth,City,Name;
NOTE: Table ORION.BIRTHMONTHS created, with 308 rows and 3 columns.

quit;
```

8

Verifying the New Table

```
proc sql;
describe table orion.birthmonths;
select * from orion.birthmonths;
quit;
```

The DESCRIBE statement writes information about the table to the SAS log.

```
proc sql;
describe table orion.birthmonths;
NOTE: SQL table ORION.BIRTHMONTHS was created like:

create table ORION.BIRTHMONTHS( bufsize=8192 )
  (
   Name char(40) format=$25.,
   City char(30) format=$25.,
   BirthMonth num format=3. label='Birth Month'
  );
```

s107d01

9

Verifying the New Table

```
proc sql;
describe table orion.birthmonths;
select * from orion.birthmonths;
quit;
```

The SELECT statement creates a report that lists the contents of the table.

Partial PROC SQL Output

Name	City	Birth Month
Aisbitt, Sandy	Melbourne	1
Sheedy, Sherie	Melbourne	1
Tannous, Cos	Melbourne	1
Boocks, Michael. R.	Miami-Dade	1
Chinnis, Kumar	Miami-Dade	1

s107d01

10

7.01 Quiz

What other Base SAS procedures are similar to the
PROC SQL DESCRIBE and SELECT statements?

11

Business Scenario: Method 2

Management wants a table for new sales staff that is
structured like the **orion.sales** table.

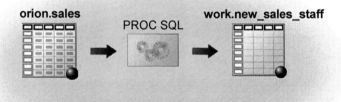

13

Creating a Table: Method 2

Copy the table structure from an existing table with the LIKE clause.

> **CREATE TABLE** *table-name-2*
> **LIKE** *table-name-1*;

```
proc sql;
create table work.new_sales_staff
    like orion.sales;
quit;
```

Name the source table.

Partial SAS Log

```
proc sql;
create table work.new_sales_staff
  like orion.sales;
NOTE: Table WORK.NEW_SALES_STAFF created, with 0 rows and 9 columns.
quit;
```

14   s107d02

Use this method when the table that you want to create is structurally identical to an existing table.

Business Scenario: Method 3

You need to create a new table to contain discount information. The structure and data needed are not in an existing table.

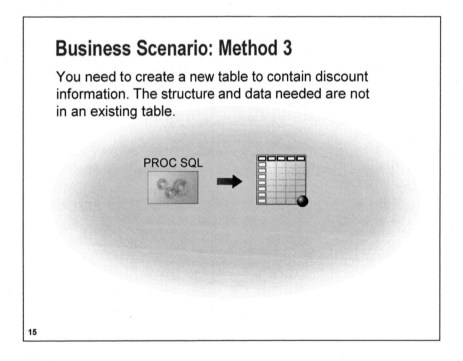

PROC SQL

15

Creating a Table: Method 3

Define the columns in the CREATE TABLE statement.

CREATE TABLE *table-name*
    (*column-name type(length)*
      <, ...*column-name type(length)*>);

```
proc sql;
create table discounts
    (Product_ID num format=z12.,
     Start_Date date,
     End_Date date,
     Discount num format=percent.);
quit;
```

The table definition is enclosed in parentheses.
Individual column definitions are separated by commas.

16   s107d03

Use this method when you create a table unlike any other existing table.

Viewing the Log

Partial SAS Log

```
proc sql;
create table discounts
    (Product_ID num format=z12.,
     Start_Date date,
     End_Date date,
     Discount num format=percent.);
NOTE: Table WORK.DISCOUNTS created, with 0 rows and 4 columns.
quit;
```

17

Defining Columns

For ANSI compliance, PROC SQL accepts the following data types in table definitions:

ANSI Type	Resulting SAS Type	Default Length	Default Format
CHAR(n)	Character	8	$w.
VARCHAR(n)	Character	8	$w.
INTEGER	Numeric	8	BEST.
SMALLINT	Numeric	8	BEST.
DECIMAL	Numeric	8	BEST.
NUMERIC	Numeric	8	BEST.
FLOAT	Numeric	8	BEST.
REAL	Numeric	8	BEST.
DOUBLE PRECISION	Numeric	8	BEST.
DATE	Numeric	8	DATE.

18

Setup for the Poll

Submit the program **s107a01** and review the SAS log.

```
proc sql;
create table discounts
    (Product_ID num format=z12.,
     Start_Date date,
     End_Date date,
     Discount num format=percent.);
describe table discounts;
quit;
```

s107a01

19

7.02 Multiple Choice Poll

Based on the query in program **s107a01**, which different data types does the **work.discounts** table have?

a. All columns are numeric type.

b. Some columns are date type and some are numeric type.

c. Some columns are character type and some are numeric type.

d. Some columns are character type, some are date type, and some are numeric type.

20

Creating Tables with PROC SQL: Job Aid

Multiple techniques are used to create tables with SQL.

Method	Description	Syntax
1	Create a table and add data all in one step, using a query.	**CREATE TABLE** *table-name* **AS SELECT...;**
2	Create an empty table by copying column attributes from an existing table using a LIKE clause.	**CREATE TABLE** *table-name* **LIKE** *old-table-name*;
3	Create an empty table by manually specifying all column attributes.	**CREATE TABLE** *table-name* (*column-name type(length)* <, ...*column-name type(length)*>);

22

If you define a column of type integer, smallint, real, or double precision and you specify a length, do not include the length value in parentheses. For those data types, the syntax is as follows:

```
column-name type n,…
```

Loading the Data

Now that you have created the empty **discounts** table, it is time to add data to it.

You need to choose the appropriate technique for adding data into this table.

24

Adding Data to a Table

The INSERT statement can be used to add data to an empty table, or to append data to a table that already contains data, using one of three methods.

Method	Description	Syntax
A	One clause per row using column-value pairs	**INSERT INTO** *table-name* **SET** *column-name=value,* *column-name=value,...;*
B	One clause per row using positional values	**INSERT INTO** *table-name* *<(column list)>* **VALUES** (*value,value,...*);
C	A query returning multiple rows based on positional values	**INSERT INTO** *table-name* *<(column list)>* **SELECT** *columns* **FROM** *table-name*;

25

The order of the values in the query expression must match the order of the column names in the insert column list or, if no list was specified, the order of the columns in the table.

Method A: Adding Data with a SET Clause

The SET clause requires that you add data using column name-value pairs:

> INSERT INTO *table-name*
> **SET** *column-name=value,*
> *column-name=value,...;*

```
insert into discounts
   set Product_ID=230100300006,
       Start_Date='01MAR2013'd,
       End_Date='15MAR2013'd,Discount=.33
   set Product_ID=230100600018,
       Start_Date='16MAR2013'd,
       End_Date='31MAR2013'd, Discount=.15;
```

26   s107d04

Method B: Adding Data with a VALUES Clause

The VALUES clause adds data to the columns in a single row of data.

> INSERT INTO *table-name*
> *<(column list)>*
> **VALUES** *(value,value,...) ;*

```
insert into discounts
   values (230100300006,'01MAR2013'd,
           '15MAR2013'd,.33)
   values (230100600018,'16MAR2013'd,
           '31MAR2013'd,.15) ;
```

 The VALUES clause must list values in the same order in which the columns are defined in the table.

27   s107d05

Method B: Adding Data with a VALUES Clause

Optionally, the INSERT statement can list the columns
into which data is to be inserted, in the order in which the
VALUES clause will provide the data.

> INSERT INTO *table-name*
> <*(column list)*>
> VALUES (*value,value,...*) ;

```
insert into discounts
(Start_Date,End_Date, Product_ID, Discount)
    values ('01MAR2013'd,'15MAR2013'd,
            230100300006,.33)
    values ('16MAR2013'd,'31MAR2013'd,
            230100600018,.15);
```

The order of the columns in the column list is independent
of the order of the columns in the table.

28   s107d05

Method C: Adding Data with a Query

Rows returned by the query are inserted into the table. If
the table has existing rows, the new rows are appended.

> INSERT INTO *table-name*
> <*(column list)*>
> SELECT *columns*
> FROM *table-name*;

```
proc sql;
insert into discounts
    (Product_ID,Discount,Start_Date,End_Date)
    select distinct Product_ID,.35,
            '01MAR2013'd,'31MAR2013'd
        from orion.Product_Dim
        where Supplier_Name contains
                'Pro Sportswear Inc';
quit;
```

⚠ The query must list values in the same order as the
INSERT statement column list.

29   s107d06

7.03 Quiz

Locate three syntax errors in the following code:

```
proc sql;
create table discounts
   (Product_ID num format=z12.,
    Start_Date date, End_Date date,
    Discount num format=percent.)
insert into discounts
   (Product_ID,Start_Date,End_Date Discount)
   values (220200200022,'01Mar2013'd,
           '31Mar2013'd,.35)
   values (220200200024,'01Mar2013'd,
           '31Mar2013'd, '.35');
quit;
```

30

Exercises

If you restarted your SAS session since the last exercise, open and submit the **libname.sas** program found in the data folder.

Level 1

1. **Creating a Table and Adding Data Using a Query**

   a. Create a table containing the following columns and name it **orion.employees**::
      - **Employee_ID**
      - **Hire_Date**
      - **Salary**
      - **Birth_Date**
      - **Gender**
      - **Country**
      - **City**

      Format all date columns with **MMDDYY10.** and **Salary** with **COMMA12.2.** Include only current employees (rows where **Employee_Term_Date** is missing). Order the output by the year value of **Hire_Date** (a variable that is not included in the output table) and then by descending **Salary**. The data that you need can be obtained from these tables:
      - **orion.employee_addresses**
      - **orion.employee_payroll**

Column Sourcing Information

Employees	Employee_Addresses	Employee_Payroll
Employee_ID	Employee_ID	Employee_ID
Hire_Date	-	Employee_Hire_Date
Salary	-	Salary
Birth_Date	-	Birth_Date
Gender	-	Employee_Gender
Country	Country	-
City	City	-

b. Query the new table **orion.employees** to produce the following report:

Partial PROC SQL Output

```
Employee_
       ID   Hire_Date      Salary  Birth_Date  Gender  Country  City

   121141   01/01/1978  194,885.00  06/19/1948  M       US       Philadelphia
   120659   01/01/1978  161,290.00  07/16/1953  M       US       Philadelphia
   120103   01/01/1978   87,975.00  01/22/1953  M       AU       Sydney
   120712   01/01/1978   63,640.00  06/12/1953  F       US       Miami-Dade
   120804   01/01/1978   55,400.00  02/11/1948  M       US       Miami-Dade
```

Level 2

2. Creating a Table by Defining Its Structure and Adding Data

a. Create a table named **orion.rewards** with four columns:

- **Purchased** – a numeric column, formatted to be nine characters wide, including commas and two decimal places

- **Year** – a numeric column, formatted to be four characters wide with no decimal places

- **Level** – a character column, which holds the value *Silver*, *Gold*, or *Platinum*

- **Award** – a character column (maximum of 50 characters)

b. Add six rows of data to the **orion.rewards** table, and then write a query to display the contents of the **Rewards** table. The results should resemble the following:

PROC SQL Output

```
Purchased  Year  Level     Award

   200.00  2012  Silver    25% Discount on one item over $25
   300.00  2012  Gold      15% Discount on one order over $50
   500.00  2012  Platinum  10% Discount on all 2012 purchases
   225.00  2013  Silver    25% Discount on one item over $50
   350.00  2013  Gold      15% Discount on one order over $100
   600.00  2013  Platinum  10% Discount on all 2013 purchases
```

Challenge

3. **Creating a Table and Inserting Data Using a Complex Query**

   Create a table named **direct_compensation** in the **work** library. The table should contain the
   following information for all *non-managerial* Sales staff (those with a level listed in their titles),
   formatted as indicated:

Employee_ID	Name	Level	Salary	Commission	Direct_ Compensation
12345	First Last	(I, II, III or IV)	12,345.00	1,234.00	13,579.00

- Sales information is available in **orion.order_fact**.
- The table **orion.sales** contains **Employee_ID**, **First_Name**, **Last_Name**, **Job_Title**, and **Salary**
  information for all Sales staff.
- **Job_Title** contains level information for each employee.
- To calculate **Commission**, add the **Total_Retail_Price** values for all sales made by an employee
  with an order date in 2011, and take 15% of that total value as commission.
- To calculate **Direct_Compensation**, add **Commission** plus **Salary**.

Partial PROC SQL Output

Employee_ID	Name	Level	Salary	Commission	Direct_ Compensation
121029	Kuo-Chung Mcelwee	I	27,225.00	3.53	27,228.53
121135	Tammy Ruta	I	27,010.00	24.12	27,034.12
120131	Marinus Surawski	I	26,910.00	59.82	26,969.82
120130	Kevin Lyon	I	26,955.00	11.10	26,966.10
121086	John-Michael Plybon	I	26,820.00	24.08	26,844.08
120136	Atul Leyden	I	26,605.00	13.88	26,618.88
120124	Lucian Daymond	I	26,480.00	132.02	26,612.02
121028	William Smades	I	26,585.00	10.41	26,595.41
120152	Sean Dives	I	26,515.00	2.87	26,517.87
121109	Harold Boulus	I	26,035.00	18.25	26,053.25
121051	Glorina Myers	I	26,025.00	18.76	26,043.77
121106	James Hilburger	I	25,880.00	2.54	25,882.54

7.2 Creating Views with the SQL Procedure

Objectives

- Create a PROC SQL view.
- Use PROC SQL views in SQL queries.
- Use PROC SQL views in other SAS procedures.
- Make a PROC SQL view portable.

37

Business Scenario

Tom Zhou is a sales manager who needs access to personnel information for his staff.

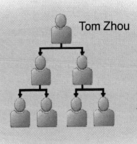

Tom Zhou

38

Business Data

The data that Tom needs is name, job title, salary, and years of service. This data is contained in three tables.

 orion.employee_addresses

 orion.employee_payroll

 orion.employee_organization

39

Considerations

What is the best way to help Tom, given the following requirements:

- He should not be allowed access to personnel data for any employee that is not his direct report.
- He can write simple PROC SQL queries and use basic SAS procedures, but cannot write complex joins.

A PROC SQL view accessing data for Tom Zhou's direct reports can provide the information that Tom needs in a secure manner.

40

What Is a PROC SQL View?

A *PROC SQL view*

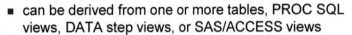

- is a stored query
- contains no actual data
- can be derived from one or more tables, PROC SQL views, DATA step views, or SAS/ACCESS views
- extracts underlying data each time it is used and accesses the most current data
- can be referenced in SAS programs in the same way as a data table
- cannot have the same name as a data table stored in the same SAS library.

41

PROC SQL views are sometimes referred to as *virtual tables* because they are referenced in SAS programs in the same manner as actual data tables, but they are not data tables. They contain no actual data. Instead, they store the instructions required to retrieve and present the data to which they refer.

Creating a PROC SQL View

To create a PROC SQL view, use the CREATE VIEW statement.

> **CREATE VIEW** *view-name* **AS**
> **SELECT ...;**

```
proc sql;
create view orion.tom_zhou as
   select Employee_Name as Name format=$25.0,
          Job_Title as Title format=$15.0,
          Salary 'Annual Salary' format=comma10.2,
          int((today()-Employee_Hire_Date)/365.25)
             as YOS 'Years of Service'
      from employee_addresses as a,
           employee_payroll as p,
           employee_organization as o
      where a.Employee_ID=p.Employee_ID and
            o.Employee_ID=p.Employee_ID and
            Manager_ID=120102;
quit;
```

42   s107d07

View the Log

Partial SAS Log

```
16    proc sql;
17    create view orion.tom_zhou as
18       select Employee_Name as Name format=$25.0,
19              Job_Title as Title format=$15.0,
20              Salary 'Annual Salary' format=comma10.2,
21              int((today()-Employee_Hire_Date)/365.25)
22                 as YOS 'Years of Service'
23          from employee_addresses as a,
24               employee_payroll as p,
25               employee_organization as o
26          where a.Employee_ID=p.Employee_ID and
27                o.Employee_ID=p.Employee_ID and
28                Manager_ID=120102;
NOTE: SQL view ORION.TOM_ZHOU has been defined.
```

43

Within any SAS library, a view cannot have the same name as an existing table, nor can a table be created with the same name as an existing view.

Location of a PROC SQL View

ANSI standards specify that the view must reside in the same SAS library as the contributing table or tables.

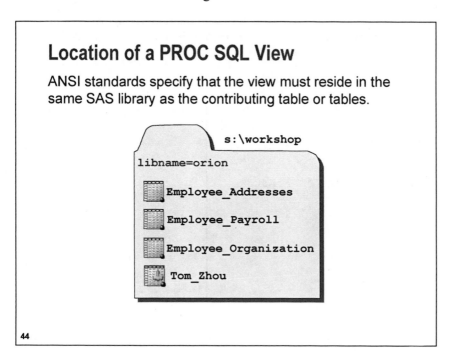

44

Location of the Source Tables: ANSI

In PROC SQL, the default libref for the table (or tables) in the FROM clause is the libref of the library that contains the view. When the view and data source are in the same location, you specify a one-level name for the table (or tables) in the FROM clause.

```
create view orion.tom_zhou as
   ...
   from employee_addresses as a,
        employee_payroll as p,
        employee_organization as o
```

45

Using the one-level name in this instance does not indicate the tables are in the SAS **work** library. As this is PROC SQL, this indicates that the tables will be in the same physical location as the view.

A PROC SQL view can be used when the physical location of the view and the underlying data are not collocated. The code in the view will use the traditional two-level names for the tables, and an additional clause, the USING clause, will be added.

Setup for Poll

Open and submit **s107a02**. View the results in the log.

Did either PROC SQL step successfully create a PROC SQL view?

46

7.04 Multiple Choice Poll

Did either PROC SQL step successfully create a PROC SQL view?

○ Yes
○ No

47   s107a02

Using a View

Tom can use the view to produce simple reports.

```
title "Tom Zhou's Direct Reports";
title2 "By Title and Years of Service";
select *
   from orion.tom_zhou
   order by Title desc, YOS desc;
```

Partial PROC SQL Output (executed 05SEP2012)

```
                   Tom Zhou's Direct Reports
                   By Title and Years of Service

                                            Annual   Years of
Name                      Title              Salary   Service

Nowd, Fadi                Sales Rep. IV    30,660.00       34
Hofmeister, Fong          Sales Rep. IV    32,040.00       29
Phoumirath, Lynelle       Sales Rep. IV    30,765.00       22
Platts, Alexei            Sales Rep. IV    32,490.00       10
```

49   s107d08

✎   **Years of Service** will change because the TODAY function was used when creating the view.

Using a View

Tom can also use the view to produce simple descriptive statistics to help him better manage his group.

```
title "Tom Zhou's Group - Salary Statistics";
proc means data=orion.tom_zhou min mean max;
   var salary;
   class title;
run;
```

PROC MEANS Output

```
             Tom Zhou's Group - Salary Statistics
                    The MEANS Procedure
           Analysis Variable : Salary Annual Salary

Title                N Obs   Minimum      Mean    Maximum

Sales Rep. I            18  25185.00  26466.67  27260.00
Sales Rep. II           13  26165.00  27123.46  28100.00
Sales Rep. III          12  28135.00  29895.42  36605.00
Sales Rep. IV            5  30660.00  31369.00  32490.00
```

s107d08

50

Business Scenario

You created a PROC SQL view to provide Tom Zhou access to personnel data for his direct reports.

Tom copied his view to a folder on his hard drive. Now Tom reports that the view does not work anymore, and he asked for your help to resolve the problem.

51

Exploring the Problem

Tom submitted the following:

```
libname orion 'c:\temp';
proc sql;
title "Tom Zhou's Direct Reports";
title2 "By Title and Years of Service";
select *
   from orion.tom_zhou
   order by Title desc, YOS desc;
quit;
title;
```

52   s107d09

Viewing the Log

Partial SAS Log

```
    libname orion 'c:\temp';
NOTE: Libref ORION was successfully assigned as follows:
      Engine:        V9
      Physical Name: c:\temp
    proc sql;
    title "Tom Zhou's Direct Reports";
    title2 "By Title and Years of Service";
    select *
       from orion.tom_zhou
       order by Title desc, YOS desc;
ERROR: File ORION.EMPLOYEE_ADDRESSES.DATA does not exist.
ERROR: File ORION.EMPLOYEE_PAYROLL.DATA does not exist.
ERROR: File ORION.EMPLOYEE_ORGANIZATION.DATA does not
exist.
    quit;
    title;
NOTE: The SAS System stopped processing this step because
of errors.
```

53

Considerations

Tom moved his view to his C:\TEMP folder and redefined the **orion** library there. This violated the one-level naming convention in the FROM clause in the view code.

```
libname orion 'c:\temp';
proc sql;
title "Tom Zhou's Direct Reports";
title2 "By Title and Years of Service";
select *
   from orion.tom_zhou
   order by Title desc, YOS desc;
quit;
```

54

Making a View Portable

> **CREATE VIEW** *view* **AS SELECT...**
>   **<USING** *LIBNAME-clause<, ...LIBNAME-clause>>*;

```
create view orion.Tom_Zhou as
   select Employee_Name as Name format=$25.0,
          Job_Title as Title format=$15.0,
          Salary "Annual Salary" format=comma10.2,
          int((today()-Employee_Hire_Date)/365.25)
             as YOS 'Years of Service'
      from orion.employee_addresses as a,
           orion.employee_payroll as p,
           orion.employee_organization as o
      where a.Employee_ID=p.E
            o.Employee_ID=p.E
            Manager_ID=120102
      using libname orion "s:\workshop";
```

two-level data set names

A USING clause names the location of the tables.

s107d10

55

If tables referenced in the FROM clause reside in different libraries, multiple LIBNAME statements can be specified in the USING clause, separated by commas. For example:

```
create view xyz as
   select <...>
   from one.a, two.b
   where <...>
   using libname one 'c:\...',
         libname two 'd:\...';
```

Validating the View

```
describe view orion.tom_zhou;
```

Partial SAS Log

```
describe view orion.tom_zhou;
NOTE: SQL view ORION.TOM_ZHOU is defined as:

        select Employee_Name as Name format=$25.0,
               Job_Title as Title format=$15.0,
               Salary label='Annual Salary' format=COMMA10.2,
               INT((TODAY() - Employee_Hire_Date) / 365.25)
                   as YOS label='Years of Service'
        from orion.employee_addresses a,
             orion.employee_payroll p,
             orion.employee_organization o
        where a.Employee_ID = p.Employee_ID and
              o.Employee_ID = p.Employee_ID and
              Manager_ID= 120102
        using libname orion "s:\workshop";
```

56   s107d10

Two-Level Table Names in Permanent Views

CREATE VIEW *proc-sql-view* **AS SELECT** ...
    <USING *LIBNAME-clause*<, ...*LIBNAME-clause*>>;

- The USING clause libref is local to the view, and it will not conflict with an identically named libref in the SAS session.
- When the query finishes, the libref is disassociated.

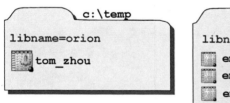

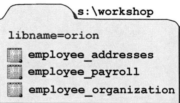

57

7.05 Quiz

What differences are there between the SQL code written
to the SAS log by the DESCRIBE VIEW statement and
the CREATE VIEW code, which actually created the view
orion.tom_zhou?

58

7.06 Poll

Considering the differences discussed in the previous
quiz, if you submit the code produced by the DESCRIBE
VIEW statement, would the view produced be identical to
the original view?

O Yes

O No

63

Views: Advantages

You can use views to do the following:

- avoid storing copies of large tables.
- avoid a frequent refresh of table copies. When the underlying data changes, a view surfaces the most current data.
- pull together data from multiple database tables and multiple libraries or databases.
- simplify complex queries.
- prevent other users from inadvertently altering the query code.

65

Views: Disadvantages

- Because views access the most current data in changing tables, the results might be different each time you access the view.
- Views can require significant resources each time that they execute. With a view, you save disk storage space at the cost of extra CPU and memory usage.
- When accessing the same data several times in a program, use a table instead of a view. This ensures consistent results from one step to the next and can significantly reduce the resources that are required.

66

General Guidelines for Creating Views

- Avoid ORDER BY clauses in view definitions, which force data sorting each time that the view is referenced.
- When you create a permanent view with permanent tables in the FROM clause, use a USING clause to specify the location of the libraries to make your view portable.

67

Exercises

If you restarted your SAS session since the last exercise, open and submit the **libname.sas** program found in the data folder.

Level 1

4. **Creating and Using a View**

   a. Create a view named **orion.phone_list** containing the following columns:
   - **Department** (format=$25.)
   - **Name** (format=$25.)
   - **Phone_Number** (label=**'Home Phone'** and format=$16.)

   Use data found in the following tables. (Columns of interest are in parentheses.)
   - **orion.employee_addresses (Employee_ID, Employee_Name)**
   - **orion.employee_organization (Employee_ID, Department)**
   - **orion.employee_phones (Employee_ID, Phone_Number, Phone_Type)**

   Include only those phone number records where **Phone_Type="Home"**.

   b. Use the new **orion.phone_list** view as the source for a query that produces the phone list for the Engineering Department, sorted by **Name**. Add this title to the report: **Engineering Department Home Phone Numbers**.

PROC SQL Output

```
                    Engineering Department Home Phone Numbers

          Name                        Home Phone

          Arizmendi, Gilbert          +1(619)551-0293
          Elleman, Lal                +61(2)5555-4127
          Elmoslamy, Wilson           +1(619)551-0291
          Hargrave, Seco              +1(215)551-0289
          Hartshorn, Darshi           +61(2)5555-2265
          Liguori, Donelle            +1(305)551-0290
          Mccleary, Bill              +61(3)5555-9767
          Peiris, Krishna             +61(2)5555-5585
          Sullivan, Lutezenia         +1(305)551-0292
```

Level 2

5. **Creating and Using a View to Provide Consolidated Information**

   a. Create a view named **orion.t_shirts** containing the following columns:

      - **Product_ID**
      - **Supplier_Name** (formatted as $20.)
      - **Product_Name**
      - **Price** (label it **Retail Price**.)

      Use data from the following tables. (Columns of interest are in parentheses.)

      - **orion.product_dim** (**Product_ID**, **Product_Name**, **Supplier_Name**)
      - **orion.price_list** (**Product_ID**, **Unit_Sales_Price**)

      Select only those records where **Product_Name** includes the word **T-Shirt**.

   b. Write a query to display the data from your new **orion.t_shirts** view. Sort the report by **Supplier_Name** and **Product_ID**. Supply a useful title.

      Partial PROC SQL Output

```
                              Available T-Shirts

      Product ID   Supplier Name       Product Name              Retail Price

      210201000050 3Top Sports         Kid Children's T-Shirt         $19.60
      240500200016 3Top Sports         T-Shirt                        $31.70
      220101300001 A Team Sports       T-Shirt, Short-sleeved,        $33.60
                                       Big Logo
      220101300012 A Team Sports       Men's T-Shirt Small Logo       $19.40
      220101300017 A Team Sports       Toncot Beefy-T                 $16.60
                                       Emb T-Shirt
```

   c. Write a query using your new **orion.t_shirts** view to display **Product_ID**, **Product_Name**, and **Price** for all T-shirts priced less than $20.00. Sort the report by price. Supply a useful title.

PROC SQL Output

```
                             T-Shirts under $20

                                                              Retail
            Product ID  Product Name                          Price

            220101300017  Toncot Beefy-T Emb T-Shirt          $16.60
            220101300012  Men's T-Shirt Small Logo            $19.40
            210201000050  Kid Children's T-Shirt              $19.60
```

Challenge

6. **Creating and Using a View That Updates Itself over Time**

   a. Create a view named **orion.current_catalog**. The view must contain all of the columns in **orion.product_dim** and a new column named **Price** (labeled **Current Retail Price**). Use data found in the following tables:

      - **orion.product_dim**

      - **orion.price_list**

      The value of the current price (**Price**) is determined by multiplying the original value of **Unit_Sales_Price** by the number of years since the product was first offered and then by the inflation factor (**Factor**). Calculate the number of years that a product was offered by subtracting the year in which the product was first offered from the current year. **Factor** is a percentage of the original price. The formula is shown below:

      Price=Unit_Sales_Price *
      (Factor(year(Today())-year(Start_Date)))**

      Round the calculated price to the nearest cent.

   b. Write a query to display **Supplier_Name**, **Product_Name**, and **Price** from your new **orion.current_catalog** view for products with **Roller Skate** in the product name. Sort the output by supplier name and price. Supply a useful title for your report. If the current year is later than 2012, your results will differ because prices have increased.

      Partial PROC SQL Output

```
                          Current Roller Skate Prices

                                                              Current
        Supplier Name              Product Name             Retail Price

        Magnifico Sports           Children's Roller Skates       $102.40
        Magnifico Sports           Pro-roll Lazer Roller Skates   $113.20
        Magnifico Sports           Pro-roll Sabotage-Rp  Roller Skates  $175.90
```

   c. Write a query to display **Product_Name**, the original value of **Unit_Sales_Price** (formerly **Price**), the current value of **Price**, and the amount of increase (**Increase** calculated as **Price–Unit_Sales_Price**) for all products having an increase greater than $5.00. Sort the report by decreasing **Increase**. Supply a useful title. If the current year is later than 2012, your results will differ because prices have increased.

Partial PROC SQL Output

2012 prices > $5.00 higher than original price			
Product Name	Old Price	New Price	Increase
Twain Ac7/Ft7 Men's Roller Skates	$181.30	$186.74	$5.44
Top R&D Long Jacket	$536.30	$541.66	$5.36

7.3 Solutions

Solutions to Exercises

1. **Creating a Table and Adding Data Using a Query**

   a.

```
*** s107s01 ***;

  /* a. */
proc sql;
create table orion.employees as
   select a.Employee_ID,
          Employee_Hire_Date as Hire_Date
          format=mmddyy10.,
          Salary format=comma12.2,
          Birth_Date format=mmddyy10.,
          Employee_Gender as Gender,
          Country, City
      from orion.employee_addresses as a,
          orion.employee_payroll as p
      where a.Employee_ID=p.Employee_ID
          and Employee_Term_Date is missing
      order by year(Hire_Date), salary desc;
quit;
```

   b.

```
  /* b. */
title;
proc sql;
select *
   from orion.employees;
quit;
```

2. **Creating a Table by Defining Its Structure and Adding Data**

   a.

```
*** s107s02 ***;
  /* a. */
proc sql;
create table orion.rewards
   (Purchased num format=comma9.2,
    Year num format=4., Level char(9),
```

```
     Award char(50));
quit;
```

b.

```
    /* b. */
proc sql;
insert into orion.rewards (Year,Level,Purchased,Award)
    values (2012,'Silver',200,'25% Discount on one item over $25')
    values (2012,'Gold',300,'15% Discount on one order over $50')
    values (2012,'Platinum',500,'10% Discount on all 2012
            purchases')
    values (2013,'Silver',225,'25% Discount on one item over $50')
    values (2013,'Gold',350,'15% Discount on one order over $100')
    values (2013,'Platinum',600,'10% Discount on all 2013
            purchases');
quit;
proc sql;
select *
  from orion.rewards;
quit;
    /*************************************************
    Alternate method - add the data using set clauses
proc sql;
insert into orion.rewards
    set year=2012,Level='Silver',Purchased=200,
        Award='25% Discount on one item over $25'
    set year=2012,Level='Gold',Purchased=300,
        Award='15% Discount on one order over $50'
    set year=2012,Level='Platinum',Purchased=500,
        Award='10% Discount on all 2012 purchases'
    set year=2013,Level='Silver',Purchased=225,
        Award='25% Discount on one item over $50'
    set year=2013,Level='Gold',Purchased=350,
        Award='15% Discount on one order over $100'
    set year=2013,Level='Platinum',Purchased=600,
        Award='10% Discount on all 2013 purchases';
quit;
    *************************************************/
```

3. Creating a Table and Inserting Data Using a Complex Query

```
    *** s107s03 ***;

proc sql;
create table work.direct_compensation as
    select hr.Employee_ID,
           catx(' ',First_Name,Last_Name) as Name,
           scan(Job_Title,-1) format=$3. as Level,
           Salary format=comma12.2,
           Sales*0.15  format=comma7.2 as Commission,
           Salary+calculated Commission format=comma12.2
              as Direct_Compensation
```

```
        from orion.sales as hr,
             (select Employee_ID,
                     sum(Total_Retail_Price) as Sales
                from orion.order_fact
                where year(Order_Date)=2011
                group by Employee_ID) as s
        where hr.Employee_ID=s.Employee_ID
              and Job_Title like ('%Rep%');
select *
   from work.direct_compensation
   order by Level, Direct_Compensation desc;
quit;
```

4. Creating and Using a View

a.

```
*** s107s04 ***;

  /* a. */
proc sql;
create view orion.phone_list as
   select Department format=$25.,
          Employee_Name as Name format=$25.0,
          Phone_Number 'Home Phone' format=$16.
      from orion.employee_addresses as a,
           orion.employee_phones as p,
           orion.employee_organization as o
      where a.Employee_ID=p.Employee_ID and
            o.Employee_ID=p.Employee_ID and
            Phone_Type="Home";
quit;
```

b.

```
  /* b. */
proc sql;
title "Engineering Department Home Phone Numbers";
select Name, Phone_Number
   from orion.lhone_list
   where Department="Engineering"
   order by Name;
quit;
title;
```

5. Creating and Using a View to Provide Consolidated Information

a.

```
*** s107s05 ***;

 /* a. */
proc sql;
create view orion.t_shirts as
   select d.Product_ID, Supplier_Name format=$20.,
```

```
              Product_Name,
              Unit_Sales_Price as Price 'Retail Price'
        from orion.product_dim as d, orion.price_list as l
        where d.Product_ID=l.Product_ID
              and lowcase(Product_Name) like '%t-shirt%';
quit;
```

b.

```
   /* b. */
proc sql flow=6 35;
title "Available T-Shirts";
select *
   from orion.t_shirts
   order by Supplier_Name, Product_ID;
quit;
title;
```

c.

```
   /* c. */
proc sql;
title "T-Shirts under $20";
select Product_ID, Product_Name, Price format=dollar6.2
   from orion.t_shirts
   where Price < 20
   order by Price;
quit;
title;
```

6. **Creating and Using a View That Updates Itself over Time**

a.

```
*** s107s06 ***;
  /* a. */
proc sql;
create view orion.current_catalog as
   /*orion.product_dim includes duplicate records*/
   select distinct d.*,
           round((l.Unit_Sales_Price *
             factor**(year(Today())-year( Start_Date ))),.01)
               'Current Retail Price' format=dollar13.2 as Price
     from orion.product_dim as d,
           orion.price_list as l
     where d.Product_ID=l.Product_ID;
quit;
```

b.

```
   /* b. */
proc sql;
title "Current Roller Skate Prices";
select Supplier_Name, Product_Name, Price
   from orion.current_catalog
   where lowcase(Product_Name) like '%roller skate%'
```

```
    order by Supplier_Name, Price;
quit;
title;
```

c.

```
    /* c. */
proc sql;
title "2012 prices > $5.00 higher than original price";
select c.Product_Name, Unit_Sales_Price 'Old Price',
       Price 'New Price',
       Price-Unit_Sales_Price as Increase format=dollar9.2
   from orion.current_catalog as c,
        orion.price_list as p
   where c.Product_ID=p.Product_id
         and calculated Increase gt 5
   order by Increase Desc;
quit;
title;
```

Solutions to Student Activities (Polls/Quizzes)

7.01 Quiz – Correct Answer

What other Base SAS procedures are similar to the
PROC SQL DESCRIBE and SELECT statements?

**PROC CONTENTS provides information similar to the
PROC SQL DESCRIBE statement.**

**PROC PRINT produces a report similar to the
PROC SQL SELECT statement.**

12

7.02 Multiple Choice Poll – Correct Answer

Based on the query in program **s107a01**, which different data types does the **work.discounts** table have?

a. All columns are numeric type.

b. Some columns are date type and some are numeric type.

c. Some columns are character type and some are numeric type.

d. Some columns are character type, some are date type, and some are numeric type.

SAS has only two data types: character and numeric.

In PROC SQL, if you specify the ANSI data type DATE when you create a table, the actual data type in the underlying SAS data set is numeric.

21

7.03 Quiz – Correct Answer

Locate three syntax errors in the following code:

1. **missing semicolon in the CREATE TABLE statement**
2. **missing comma in the column name list**
3. **quotation marks around numeric value in the second VALUES clause**

```
proc sql;
create table Discounts
    (Product_ID num format=z12.,
     Start_Date date, End_Date date,
     Discount num format=percent.) ;
insert into discounts
    (Product_ID,Start_Date,End_Date,Discount)
     values (220200200022,'01Mar2013'd,
             '31Mar2013'd,.35)
     values (220200200024,'01Mar2013'd,
             '31Mar2013'd, .35) ;
```

33

7.04 Multiple Choice Poll – Correct Answer

Did either PROC SQL step successfully create a PROC SQL view?

○ Yes
◉ No

The CREATE VIEW statement differs from the CREATE TABLE statement in that a view is *always* created from the results of a query. Methods that create empty tables without extracting data are not appropriate for creating views.

48

7.05 Quiz – Correct Answer

Differences between the SQL code produced by the **DESCRIBE VIEW** statement and the actual **CREATE VIEW** code, which created **orion.tom_zhou**:

Original
```
select Employee_Name as Name format=$25.0,
       Job_Title as Title format=$15.0,
       Salary 'Annual Salary' format=comma10.2,
       int((today()-Employee_Hire_Date)/365.25)
       as YOS 'Years of Service'
  from Employee_Addresses as a,Employee_Payroll as p,
       Employee_Organization as o
 where a.Employee_ID=p.Employee_ID and
       o.Employee_ID=p.Employee_ID and
       Manager_ID=120102;
```

DESCRIBE VIEW
```
select Employee_Name as Name format=$25.0,
       Job_Title as Title format=$15.0,
       Salary label='Annual Salary' format=COMMA10.2,
       int((today()-Employee_Hire_Date)/365.25)
          as YOS label='Years of Service'
  from EMPLOYEE_ADDRESSES a, EMPLOYEE_PAYROLL p,
       EMPLOYEE_ORGANIZATION o
 where (a.Employee_ID=p.Employee_ID) and
       (o.Employee_ID=p.Employee_ID) and
       (Manager_ID=120102);
```

59

continued...

7.05 Quiz – Correct Answer

Differences between the SQL code produced by the
DESCRIBE VIEW statement and the actual CREATE
VIEW code, which created **orion.tom_zhou**:

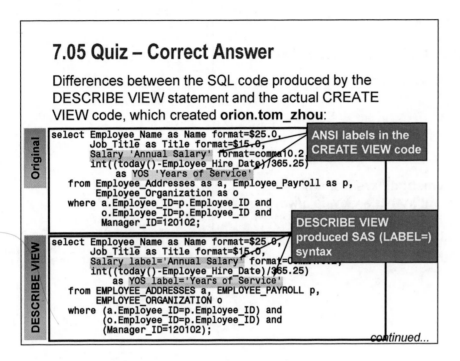

7.05 Quiz – Correct Answer

Differences between the SQL code produced by the
DESCRIBE VIEW statement and the actual CREATE
VIEW code, which created **orion.tom_zhou**:

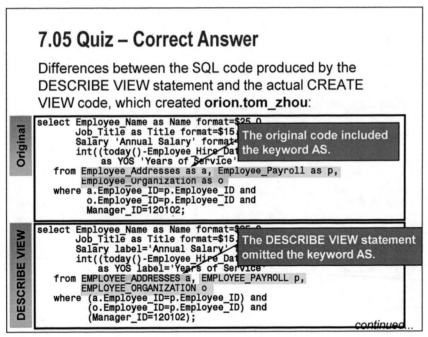

7.05 Quiz – Correct Answer

Differences between the SQL code produced by the
DESCRIBE VIEW statement and the actual CREATE
VIEW code, which created **orion.tom_zhou**:

Original
```
select Employee_Name as Name format=$25.0,
       Job_Title as Title format=$15.0,
       Salary 'Annual Salary' format=comma10.2,
       int((today()-Employee_Hire_Date)/365.25)
           as YOS 'Years of Service'
  from Employee_Addresses as a, Employee_Payroll as p,
       Employee_Organization as o
 where a.Employee_ID=p.Employee_ID and
       o.Employee_ID=p.Employee_ID and
       Manager_ID=120102;
```

DESCRIBE VIEW
```
select Employee_Name as Name format=$25.0
       Job_Title as Title format=$15.
       Salary label='Annual Salary'
       int((today()-Employee_Hire_Dat
           as YOS label='Years of Service'
  from EMPLOYEE_ADDRESSES a, EMPLOYEE_PAYROLL p,
       EMPLOYEE_ORGANIZATION o
 where (a.Employee_ID=p.Employee_ID) and
       (o.Employee_ID=p.Employee_ID) and
       (Manager_ID=120102);
```

> The DESCRIBE VIEW statement inserted parentheses.

7.06 Poll – Correct Answer

Considering the differences discussed in the previous
quiz, if you submit the code produced by the DESCRIBE
VIEW statement, would the view produced be identical to
the original view?

- ⦿ Yes
- ○ No

64

Chapter 8 Advanced PROC SQL Features

8.1 Dictionary Tables and Views

Objectives

- Use dictionary tables and views to obtain information about SAS files.

3

Business Scenario

You have inherited many different data tables and want to become familiar with their content.

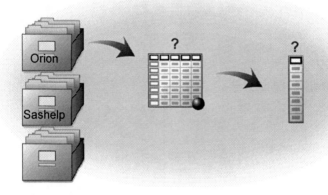

4

Dictionary Tables: Overview

Dictionary tables are Read-Only metadata views that contain session metadata, such as information about SAS libraries, data sets, and external files in use or available in the current SAS session.

Dictionary tables are

- created at SAS session initialization
- updated automatically by SAS
- limited to Read-Only access.

You can query dictionary tables with PROC SQL.

5

Metadata is data that provides information about other data.

Querying Metadata about SAS Libraries

There can be more than 30 dictionary tables. We will focus on using data from three of the tables.

DICTIONARY.TABLES
- detailed information about tables

DICTIONARY.COLUMNS
- detailed information about all columns in all tables

DICTIONARY.MEMBERS
- general information about SAS library members

6

SAS librefs are limited to eight characters. The libref **dictionary** is an automatically assigned, reserved libref that is accessible only from within PROC SQL.

Exploring Dictionary Tables

You can use a DESCRIBE statement to explore the structure of dictionary tables:

```
describe table dictionary.tables;
```

Partial Log

```
NOTE: SQL table DICTIONARY.TABLES was created like:

create table DICTIONARY.TABLES
  (
   libname char(8) label='Library Name',
   memname char(32) label='Member Name',
   ...
   crdate num format=DATETIME informat=DATETIME label='Date Created',
   modate num format=DATETIME informat=DATETIME label='Date Modified',
   nobs num label='Number of Physical Observations',
   obslen num label='Observation Length',
   nvar num label='Number of Variables', ...);
```

s108d01

7

The DESCRIBE TABLE statement is a good tool for exploring dictionary tables. The complete log notes from the DESCRIBE statement are shown below:

```
create table DICTIONARY.TABLES
  (
   libname char(8) label='Library Name',
   memname char(32) label='Member Name',
   memtype char(8) label='Member Type',
   dbms_memtype char(32) label='DBMS Member Type',
   memlabel char(256) label='Dataset Label',
   typemem char(8) label='Dataset Type',
   crdate num format=DATETIME informat=DATETIME label='Date Created',
   modate num format=DATETIME informat=DATETIME label='Date Modified',
   nobs num label='Number of Physical Observations',
   obslen num label='Observation Length',
   nvar num label='Number of Variables',
   protect char(3) label='Type of Password Protection',
   compress char(8) label='Compression Routine',
   encrypt char(8) label='Encryption',
   npage num label='Number of Pages',
   filesize num label='Size of File',
   pcompress num label='Percent Compression',
   reuse char(3) label='Reuse Space',
   bufsize num label='Bufsize',
   delobs num label='Number of Deleted Observations',
   nlobs num label='Number of Logical Observations',
   maxvar num label='Longest variable name',
   maxlabel num label='Longest label',
   maxgen num label='Maximum number of generations',
   gen num label='Generation number',
   attr char(3) label='Dataset Attributes',
   indxtype char(9) label='Type of Indexes',
   datarep char(32) label='Data Representation',
   sortname char(8) label='Name of Collating Sequence',
   sorttype char(4) label='Sorting Type',
```

```
    sortchar char(8) label='Charset Sorted By',
    reqvector char(24) format=$HEX48 informat=$HEX48 label='Requirements Vector',
    datarepname char(170) label='Data Representation Name',
    encoding char(256) label='Data Encoding',
    audit char(3) label='Audit Trail Active?',
    audit_before char(3) label='Audit Before Image?',
    audit_admin char(3) label='Audit Admin Image?',
    audit_error char(3) label='Audit Error Image?',
    audit_data char(3) label='Audit Data Image?'
);
```

Querying Dictionary Information

Display information about the tables in the **orion** library.

```
title 'Tables in the ORION Library';
proc sql;
select memname 'Table Name',
       nobs,nvar,crdate
   from dictionary.tables
   where libname='ORION';
quit;
```

Library names are stored in uppercase in dictionary tables.

s108d01

8

SAS library and table names are stored in uppercase in the dictionary tables. Using SAS functions, such as UPCASE() or LOWCASE(), when querying dictionary tables dramatically degrades query performance. For example, using **upcase(Libname)='ORION'** will cause *all* assigned librefs assigned to the SAS session to be opened to return this information. This prevents the PROC SQL Query Optimizer from seeing many conditions that could be optimized. This is especially apparent when librefs are assigned to a DBMS using a SAS/ACCESS engine.

When you query dictionary tables, you supply values to the WHERE clause in the appropriate case, and match the known case for library and table names (uppercase) and for column names (mixed case). (Know your data!)

The PRESERVE_TAB_NAMES=YES and PRESERVE_COL_NAMES=YES options change the way that some table and column names are seen by SAS in the dictionary tables. These options might require further investigation to maximize the efficiency of your queries.

Viewing the Output

Partial PROC SQL Output

```
                  Tables in the ORION Library

                     Number of
                     Physical   Number of
Table Name           Observations Variables    Date Created

CUSTOMER                   77           12   14DEC07:08:05:44
CUSTOMER_TYPE              8            4    14DEC07:08:05:42
EMPLOYEE_ADDRESSES         424          9    23OCT07:10:12:23
EMPLOYEE_DONATIONS         124          7    14JAN08:10:34:21
EMPLOYEE_INFORMATION       424          11   05JUL12:11:25:08
EMPLOYEE_ORGANIZATION      424          4    12OCT07:14:06:32
EMPLOYEE_PAYROLL           424          8    14DEC07:08:08:06
```

9

✎   This report will vary based on the tables created during class.

Querying Dictionary Information

Display information about the columns in
orion.employee_addresses.

```
title 'Columns in the orion.employee_addresses '
      'Table';
proc sql;
select Name,Type,Length
   from dictionary.columns
   where libname='ORION'
         and memname='EMPLOYEE_ADDRESSES';
quit;
```

Table names (*memnames*)
are also stored in uppercase
in dictionary tables.

10   s108d01

Viewing the Output

PROC SQL Output

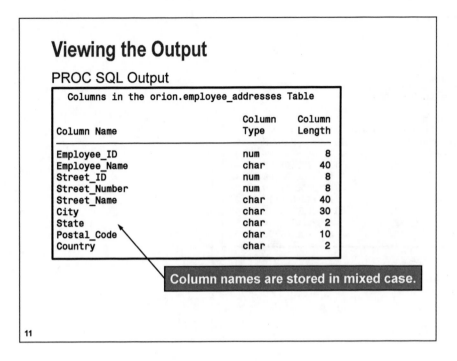

```
         Columns in the orion.employee_addresses Table

                                  Column    Column
  Column Name                     Type      Length

  Employee_ID                     num            8
  Employee_Name                   char          40
  Street_ID                       num            8
  Street_Number                   num            8
  Street_Name                     char          40
  City                            char          30
  State                           char           2
  Postal_Code                     char          10
  Country                         char           2
```

Column names are stored in mixed case.

11

Using Dictionary Information

Which tables contain the **Employee_ID** column?

```
title 'Tables Containing an Employee_ID '
      'Column';
proc sql;
select memname 'Table Names', name
   from dictionary.columns
   where libname='ORION' and
         upcase(name)='EMPLOYEE_ID';
quit;
```

Because different tables might use different cases for same-named columns, you can use the UPCASE function for comparisons. However, this significantly degrades the performance of the query.

12   s108d01

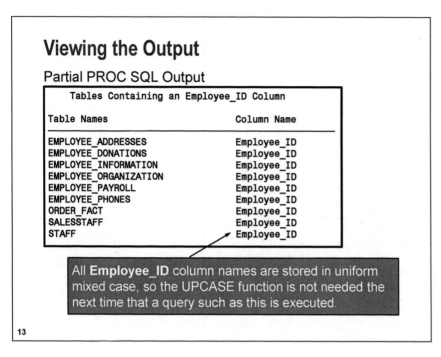

Viewing the Output

Partial PROC SQL Output

```
    Tables Containing an Employee_ID Column

Table Names                    Column Name

EMPLOYEE_ADDRESSES             Employee_ID
EMPLOYEE_DONATIONS             Employee_ID
EMPLOYEE_INFORMATION           Employee_ID
EMPLOYEE_ORGANIZATION          Employee_ID
EMPLOYEE_PAYROLL               Employee_ID
EMPLOYEE_PHONES                Employee_ID
ORDER_FACT                     Employee_ID
SALESSTAFF                     Employee_ID
STAFF                          Employee_ID
```

All **Employee_ID** column names are stored in uniform mixed case, so the UPCASE function is not needed the next time that a query such as this is executed.

13

The tables identified in this report will vary depending on the files created in your SAS session.

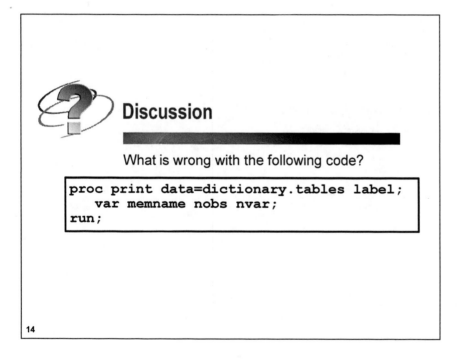

Discussion

What is wrong with the following code?

```
proc print data=dictionary.tables label;
   var memname nobs nvar;
run;
```

14

Using Dictionary Tables in Other SAS Code

SAS provides views based on the dictionary tables in the **Sashelp** library.

Most of the **Sashelp** library dictionary view names are similar to dictionary table names, but are shortened to eight characters or less. They begin with the letter v and do not end in s. For example:

dictionary.tables = sashelp.vtable

The following code executes successfully:

```
title 'Tables in the ORION Library';
proc print data=sashelp.vtable label;
   var memname nobs nvar;
   where libname='ORION';
run;
```

16   s108d02

8.01 Quiz

In your SAS session's SAS Explorer window, navigate to the **Sashelp** library by selecting **Libraries** ⇨ **Sashelp**. Scroll down to examine the **Sashelp** views.

Which view shows the names and data types of all the columns in every table available in the SAS session?

17

Business Scenario

An analyst asked for a report showing the SAS tables, views, catalogs, and other SAS objects that are in the various libraries.

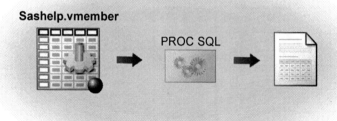

Sashelp.vmember

PROC SQL

19

Using Dictionary Information

Use **sashelp.vmember** to extract information from **dictionary.members** in a PROC TABULATE step.

```
title 'SAS Objects by Library';
proc tabulate data=sashelp.vmember format=8.;
   class libname memtype;
   keylabel N=' ';
   table libname, memtype/rts=10
         misstext='None';
   where libname in ('ORION','SASUSER',
                     'SASHELP');
run;
```

20   s108d02

Viewing the Output

PROC TABULATE Output

SAS Objects by Library

	Member Type				
	CATALOG	DATA	ITEMSTOR	MDDB	VIEW
Library Name					
ORION	None	19	None	None	4
SASHELP	132	191	2	2	38
SASUSER	3	101	1	None	1

21

 The numbers on this report might vary depending on the files that were created in your SAS session.

Exercises

If you restarted your SAS session since the last exercise, open and submit the **libname.sas** program found in the data folder.

Level 1

1. **Using PROC SQL Options and Displaying the Contents of a Dictionary Table**

   a. Write a query that retrieves **memname** (table name) and **memlabel** (description of the table) from **dictionary.dictionaries**. Include only a single row per table name displayed.
   Use the FLOW= option to ensure that columns wrap between 6 – 35 characters. Title the report **Dictionary Tables**.

   Partial PROC SQL Output

Dictionary Tables	
Member Name	Data Set Label
CATALOGS	Catalogs and catalog-specific information
CHECK_CONSTRAINTS	Check constraints
COLUMNS	Columns from every table
CONSTRAINT_COLUMN_USAGE	Constraint column usage
CONSTRAINT_TABLE_USAGE	Constraint table usage
DATAITEMS	Information Map Data Items

DESTINATIONS	Open ODS Destinations
DICTIONARIES	DICTIONARY tables and their columns
ENGINES	Available engines
EXTFILES	Files defined in FILENAME statements, or implicitly

b. Use the columns **memname, type,** and **length** from **dictionary.columns** where **libname="ORION"** and the table contains a column (**Name**) named **Customer_ID** (**upcase(Name)='CUSTOMER_ID'**). Title the report **Tables containing Customer_ID**.

PROC SQL Output

Tables containing Customer_ID		
Member Name	Column Type	Column Length
CUSTOMER	num	8
ORDER_FACT	num	8
QTR1	num	8
QTR2	num	8

Level 2

2. **Using PROC SQL Options and Displaying Dictionary Table Information**

   a. Produce a report that includes **memname** (table name), **memlabel** (table description), and a count of the number of columns in each table, by querying **dictionary.dictionaries**. Display only one row per table name. Use the FLOW= option to wrap columns between 6 – 35 characters. Title the report **Dictionary Tables**.

   Partial PROC SQL Output

Dictionary Tables		
Member Name	Data Set Label	Columns
CATALOGS	Catalogs and catalog-specific information	10
CHECK_CONSTRAINTS	Check constraints	4
COLUMNS	Columns from every table	18
CONSTRAINT_COLUMN_USAGE	Constraint column usage	7

   b. List the table name (**memname**), number of rows (**nobs**), number of columns (**nvar**), file size (**filesize**), length of the widest column (**maxvar**), and length of the widest column label (**maxlabel**) by querying **dictionary.tables**. Limit the list to tables in the **orion** library (**libname="ORION"**) and exclude views (**memtype ne 'VIEW'**) from your report. Order the report by table name. Give the columns labels as indicated by the sample output. Name the report **Orion Library Tables**. If you wrote additional tables to the **orion** library, your output might differ from the sample PROC SQL output.

   PROC SQL Output

Orion Library Tables					
Table	Rows	Columns	File Size	Widest Column	Widest Label

CUSTOMER	77	12	49152	18	19
EMPLOYEE_ADDRESSES	424	9	86016	13	0
EMPLOYEE_DONATIONS	124	7	36864	11	11
EMPLOYEE_ORGANIZATION	424	4	49152	11	0
EMPLOYEE_PAYROLL	424	8	40960	18	0
EMPLOYEE_PHONES	923	3	229376	12	11
ORDER_FACT	617	12	73728	18	48
PRICE_LIST	259	6	24576	16	24
PRODUCT_DIM	481	8	131072	16	16
QTR1	22	5	8192	13	33
QTR2	36	6	8192	13	33
SALES	165	9	32768	11	0
SALESSTAFF	163	10	36864	13	25
STAFF	424	10	57344	13	25

Challenge

3. **Using PROC SQL Options, SAS System Options, and Dictionary Tables to Document Data Tables in the Orion Star Library**

   a. Use PROC SQL options, SAS system options, and **dictionary.tables** to document the data tables in the **orion** library. In the report, exclude views and output only one row per table. For each numeric column, the query should place an asterisk beside each of the maximum values. (See the sample output below.) If you created tables in the **orion** library during this class, your output might have additional entries.

   Partial PROC SQL Output

```
                        ORION Library Table Information

                                          File Size
   Table          Rows        Columns      (Bytes)        Widest Column

   CUSTOMER        77          12*          49152          18*
   EMPLOYEE_       424         9            86016          13
   ADDRESSES
   EMPLOYEE_       124         7            36864          11
   ...
   SALESSTAFF      163         10           36864          13
   STAFF           424         10           65536          13

                        * Largest in the Library
```

   Hint: Consider using a CASE statement to generate the asterisks in the report.

8.2 Using SQL Procedure Options

Objectives

- Use SQL procedure options to control processing details.

25

PROC SQL Options

PROC SQL options give you finer control over your SQL processes by providing the following features:

- syntax checking without executing your code
- expanding SQL statements to their fully qualified values
- restricting the number of rows processed
- providing system utilization statistics for query tuning

PROC SQL *options*;

26

Business Scenario

You have been asked to produce a report of the 10 most profitable customers.

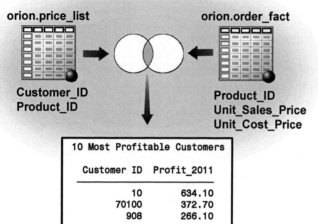

orion.price_list

Customer_ID
Product_ID

orion.order_fact

Product_ID
Unit_Sales_Price
Unit_Cost_Price

```
10 Most Profitable Customers

Customer ID   Profit_2011

          10       634.10
       70100       372.70
         908       266.10
```

27

OUTOBS= PROC SQL Option

Join all rows, but limit output to the 10 most profitable customers.

OUTOBS=*n*

```
proc sql outobs=10;
title "10 Most Profitable Customers";
select Customer_ID,
       sum(Unit_Sales_Price-Unit_Cost_Price)
       as Profit_2011 format=comma8.2
   from orion.price_list as p,
        orion.order_fact as o
   where p.Product_ID=o.Product_id
         and year(Order_date)=2011
   group by Customer_ID
   order by Profit_2011 desc;
quit;
```

s108d03

28

Viewing the Output

PROC SQL Output

```
              10 Most Profitable Customers

          Customer ID   Profit_2011

                   10        634.10
                70100        372.70
                  908        266.10
                   31        225.35
                  171        207.50
                   27        204.95
                70201        197.85
                 2806        177.95
                   34        142.65
                46966        138.80
```

29

8.02 Multiple Answer Poll

Specifying the NOEXEC option in a PROC SQL statement does which of the following?

a. prevents statement execution for the current invocation of PROC SQL

b. applies only to the SELECT statement

c. checks SQL query syntax without actually executing the statements

d. displays rewritten PROC SQL statements after references are expanded and certain other transformations are made

30

SQL Options: Controlling Processing

Option	Effect
OUTOBS=n	Restricts the number of rows that a query outputs (displays or writes to a table).
INOBS=n	Sets a limit of n rows from each source table that contributes to a query.
NOEXEC	Checks syntax for all SQL statements without executing them.

32

continued...

SQL Options: Controlling Display

Option	Effect
PRINT|NOPRINT	Controls whether the results of a SELECT statement are displayed as a report.
NONUMBER|NUMBER	Controls whether the row number is displayed as the first column in query output.

33

continued...

    The default value appears first in the slides.

The NONUMBER|NUMBER option affects only PROC SQL reports displayed in an output destination. It cannot be used to add observation numbers to data tables created using PROC SQL.

SQL Options: Controlling Display

Option	Effect
NOSTIMER|STIMER	Controls whether PROC SQL writes resource utilization statistics to the SAS log.
NODOUBLE|DOUBLE*	Controls whether the report is double-spaced.

* This option applies to the SAS LISTING destination only.

34

continued...

SQL Options: Controlling Display

Option	Effect
NOFLOW|FLOW| * FLOW=n|FLOW=n <m>	controls the appearance of wide character columns. The FLOW option causes text to flow in its column rather than wrapping an entire row. Specifying n determines the width of the flowed column. Specifying n and m floats the width of the column between the limits to achieve a balanced layout.

* This option applies to the SAS LISTING destination only.

35

INOBS= PROC SQL Option

For testing purposes, read 10n rows from **orion.price_list**.

INOBS=*n*

```
proc sql inobs=10;
title "orion.price_list - INOBS=10";
select Product_ID,
       Unit_Cost_Price format=comma8.2,
       Unit_Sales_Price format=comma8.2,
       Unit_Sales_Price-Unit_Cost_Price
       as Margin format=comma8.2
   from orion.price_list;
quit;
```

✎ The INOBS= option applies to each input table.

s108d04

36

Viewing the Output

PROC SQL Output

```
            orion.price_list - INOBS=10

                      Unit      Unit
                      Cost      Sales
         Product ID   Price     Price     Margin
         ──────────────────────────────────────────
         210200100009  15.50    34.70     19.20
         210200100017  17.80    40.00     22.20
         210200200023   8.25    19.80     11.55
         210200600067  28.90    67.00     38.10
         210200600085  17.85    39.40     21.55
         210200600112   9.25    21.80     12.55
         210200900033   6.45    14.20      7.75
         210200900038   9.30    20.30     11.00
         210201000050   9.00    19.60     10.60
         210201000126   2.30     6.50      4.20
```

37

Resetting Options

Use the RESET statement to add or change PROC SQL options without re-invoking the procedure.

> **RESET** *option(s)*;

🖊 An option specified in the PROC SQL statement remains in effect until you re-invoke PROC SQL or issue a RESET statement.

38

8.03 Quiz

Open the program **s108a01**. This SQL query joins **orion.employee_addresses** and **orion.employee_donations** to calculate each employee's total charitable contribution for 2011. Output rows are numbered and are limited to 10 observations.

Without re-invoking PROC SQL, add a statement before the second query that does the following:

- displays output rows without row numbers
- ensures that only nine rows are output

39

8.3 Interfacing PROC SQL with the Macro Language

Objectives

- State the purpose of the SAS macro language.
- Create and use SAS macro variables in PROC SQL.
- Insert information from dictionary tables into SAS macro variables to create a self-modifying SQL query.

43

Business Scenario

A manager asked you to include some report data in a report title.

```
            Sales Department Employees Earning
      More than the Department Average of 27503.06

            Row    Employee_ID    Salary

             57      121081        30235
             58      121082        28510
```

Including this type of information in a report title requires an understanding of SAS macro variables and their use in PROC SQL.

44

Creating and Referencing Macro Variables

Create macro variables and then submit code to create a report using the defined macro variables.

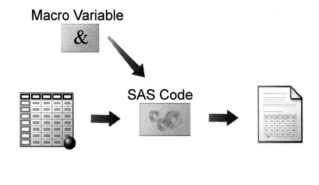

45

PROC SQL and Macro Variables

In PROC SQL, you can use *macro variables* to store values returned by a query. You can then reference macro variables in other PROC SQL statements and steps.

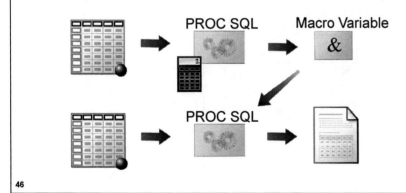

46

The SAS Macro Facility Overview

The SAS macro facility enables you to use the SAS macro language to do the following:

- create macro variables that contain text, and reference them anywhere in a SAS program.
  &

- write special programs (macros) that generate customized SAS code.
  %

47

Macro Variables

SAS macro variables are stored in an area of memory referred to as the *global symbol table*.

There are two types of macro variables: automatic (created and updated by SAS) and user-defined.

Partial Global Symbol Table

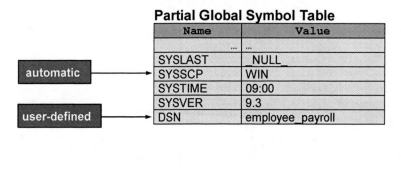

Name	Value
...	...
SYSLAST	_NULL_
SYSSCP	WIN
SYSTIME	09:00
SYSVER	9.3
DSN	employee_payroll

automatic →
user-defined →

48

The following macro statement will display all macro variables in the global symbol table. This report will be written to the SAS log.

```
%put _all_;
```

To create a report of automatic macro variables, submit the following:

```
%put _automatic_;
```

Creating and Referencing Macro Variables

Taking advantage of macro variables requires two steps.

1. Create and assign a value to a macro variable using one of these methods:
   - %LET statement in SAS code
   - INTO clause in a PROC SQL query
   - CALL SYMPUTX routine in SAS code

2. Reference the macro variable in SAS code so that SAS can resolve the macro variable value.
   - Use &*macro-name*

49

Creating Macro Variables: %LET Statement

Use the %LET macro statement to create and assign a value to a macro variable.

> **%LET** *variable=value*;

```
%let DSN=employee_payroll;
%let bigsalary=100000;
%let libname='ORION';
```

> *variable* is any valid SAS variable name, and *value* is any text string.

In SAS macro statements, most keywords are preceded by a percent sign (%).

50

The %LET statement is a global statement.

 In the %LET statement, *value* can be any string.
- Maximum length is 64K characters.
- Minimum length is 0 characters (*null value*).
- Numeric tokens are stored as character strings.
- Mathematical expressions are not evaluated.
- The case of *value* is preserved.

- Quotation marks are stored as part of *value*.
- Leading and trailing blanks are removed from *value* before the assignment is made.

Creating Macro Variables: %LET Statement

If the macro variable does not exist, then the %LET creates it and assigns it a value.

If the macro variable exists (it is in the Global Symbol table), then the %LET assigns the new value.

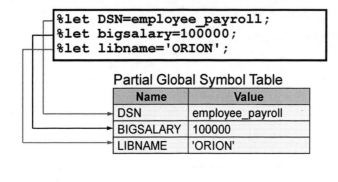

```
%let DSN=employee_payroll;
%let bigsalary=100000;
%let libname='ORION';
```

Partial Global Symbol Table

Name	Value
DSN	employee_payroll
BIGSALARY	100000
LIBNAME	'ORION'

51

Resolving Symbolic References

When the code is submitted, the second macro variable is resolved. The value is obtained from the symbol table and substituted in the program before the syntax is evaluated.

Partial Global Symbol Table

Name	Value
DSN	employee_payroll
BIGSALARY	100000
LIBNAME	'ORION'

```
proc sql;
select *
   from orion.employee_payroll
   where Salary > 100000;
```

55

Referencing a Macro Variable in Quotation Marks

To reference a macro variable within a quoted text string, enclose the reference in *double* quotation marks.

Partial Global Symbol Table

Name	Value
CITY	San Diego

A macro variable resolves within double quotation marks.

```
title "Report for &city";
```

56

Referencing a Macro Variable in Quotation Marks

To reference a macro variable within a quoted text string, enclose the reference in *double* quotation marks.

Partial Global Symbol Table

Name	Value
CITY	San Diego

A macro variable resolves within double quotation marks.

```
title "Report for &city";
```

```
title "Report for San Diego";
```

Output

```
Report for San Diego
```

57

Discussion

What happens if the macro
variable value includes quotation
marks?

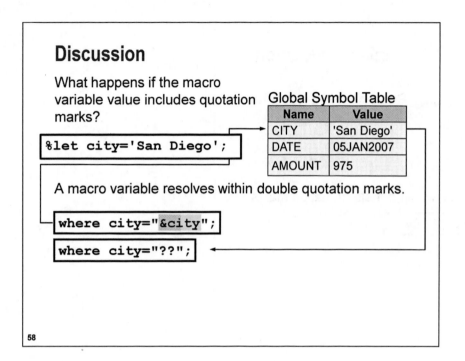

Global Symbol Table

Name	Value
CITY	'San Diego'
DATE	05JAN2007
AMOUNT	975

```
%let city='San Diego';
```

A macro variable resolves within double quotation marks.

```
where city="&city";
```

```
where city="??";
```

Referencing a Macro Variable in Quotation Marks

A macro variable within *single* quotation marks will not
resolve. The text is treated as literal, and no attempt is
made to reference the global symbol table.

```
title 'Report for &city';
```

Output

```
Report for &city
```

Business Scenario

Create macro variables and then a report using the defined macro variables. You want to validate that the macro variables work in code.

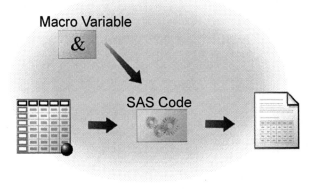

61

Displaying Macro Variable Values

Use the %PUT statement to display the resolved macro variable value along with descriptive text in the SAS log.

```
%let DSN=employee_payroll;
%let bigsalary=100000;
%put DSN is &DSN;
%put bigsalary is &bigsalary;
```

%PUT *text*;

Partial SAS Log

```
   %put DSN is &DSN;
DSN is employee_payroll
   %put bigsalary is &bigsalary;
bigsalary is 100000
```

62   s108d05

Displaying Macro Variable Values

When you submit code containing macro variable references, use the SYMBOLGEN system option to see the value that was substituted in the code echoed in the SAS log.

OPTIONS SYMBOLGEN;

```
options symbolgen;
proc sql;
title "Salaries > &bigsalary";
select  Employee_ID, Salary
   from orion.&DSN
   where Salary > &bigsalary;
quit;
```

Partial SAS Log

```
68    options symbolgen;
69    proc sql;
SYMBOLGEN:  Macro variable BIGSALARY resolves to 100000
70    title "Salaries > &bigsalary";
```

63   s108d05

✎   NOSYMBOLGEN is the default system option setting.

Validating Macro Variable Resolution

Display the results of a resolved macro variable reference in the SAS log with the SYMBOLGEN system option.

```
%let DSN=employee_payroll;
%let bigsalary=100000;
%put DSN is &DSN;
%put bigsalary is &bigsalary;
options symbolgen;
proc sql;
title "Salaries > &bigsalary";
select  Employee_ID, Salary
   from orion.&DSN
   where Salary > &bigsalary;
quit;
```

64   s108d05

Viewing the Log

Partial SAS Log

```
   %let DSN=employee_payroll;
   %let bigsalary=100000;

   %put DSN is &DSN;
DSN is employee_payroll
   %put bigsalary is &bigsalary;
bigsalary is 100000

   options symbolgen;
   proc sql;
SYMBOLGEN:  Macro variable BIGSALARY resolves to 100000
   title "Salaries > &bigsalary";
   select  Employee_ID, Salary
      from orion.&DSN
SYMBOLGEN:  Macro variable DSN resolves to employee_payroll
      where Salary
SYMBOLGEN:  Macro variable BIGSALARY resolves to 100000
  !              > &bigsalary;
```

65

Viewing the Output

PROC SQL Output

```
              Salaries > 100000

          Employee_ID    Salary

              120101    163040
              120102    108255
              120259    433800
              120260    207885
              120261    243190
              120262    268455
              120659    161290
              121141    194885
              121142    156065
```

66

Creating Macro Variables with PROC SQL

In PROC SQL, you use an INTO clause to create macro variables and assign a value to them or to update existing macro variable values. The INTO clause must follow the SELECT clause.

```
SELECT ...
    INTO ...
    FROM table|view ...
    <additional clauses>
```

The INTO clause has three syntaxes, and each produces a different result.

68

The INTO clause occurs between the SELECT list and the FROM clause. It cannot be used in a CREATE TABLE or CREATE VIEW statement. Use the NOPRINT option if you do not want to display the query result.

Business Scenario

Create a report listing all employees in the Sales Department with salaries above the department average. Include the average salary for the department in the report title.

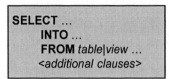

```
            Sales Department Employees Earning
    More than the Department Average of 27503.06

            Row    Employee_ID    Salary

             57       121081       30235
             58       121082       28510
             59       121085       32235
             60       121087       28325
             61       121089       28095
```

69

Creating Macro Variables: Syntax 1

Syntax 1 places values from the *first row* returned by an SQL query into one or more macro variables. Data from additional rows returned by the query is ignored.

> **SELECT** *column-1* format=*format-name.*
> <, ...*column-n*>
>   **INTO** :*macvar_1*<, ... :*macvar_n*>
>   **FROM** *table|view* ...

The value from the first column in the SELECT clause is placed in the first macro variable listed in the INTO clause, and so on.

70

This method is most often used with queries that return only one row.

 If a format is not applied to large numeric values, then the values can be stored in scientific notation.

Creating One Macro Variable: Syntax 1

Step 1 Calculate the average Sales Department salary and store the value in a macro variable.

```
%let Dept=Sales;
proc sql noprint;
select avg(Salary)
   into :MeanSalary
   from orion.employee_payroll as p,
        orion.employee_organization as o
   where p.Employee_ID=o.Employee_ID
        and Department=propcase("&Dept");
```

71   s108d06

Creating One Macro Variable: Syntax 1

Step 2 List employees in the Sales Department with salaries greater than the average. Include the average salary in the title.

```
reset print number;
title "&Dept Department Employees Earning";
title2 "More than the Department Average "
       "of &MeanSalary";
select p.Employee_ID, Salary
   from orion.employee_payroll as p,
        orion.employee_organization as o
   where p.Employee_ID=O.Employee_ID
     and Department=Propcase("&Dept")
     and Salary > &MeanSalary;
```

72   s108d06

Viewing the Output

Partial PROC SQL Output (Rows 57–69)

```
          Sales Department Employees Earning
     More than the Department Average of 27503.06

          Row    Employee_ID    Salary

           57      121081        30235
           58      121082        28510
           59      121085        32235
           60      121087        28325
           61      121089        28095
           62      121095        28010
           63      121099        32725
           64      121100        28135
           65      121104        28315
           66      121105        29545
           67      121107        31380
           68      121129        30945
           69      121139        27700
```

In the Sales Department, 69 employees earn above-average salaries.

73

8.04 Quiz

How many changes must be made to the program
to generate a report showing how many Engineering
Department employees earn above-average salaries?

```
%let Dept=Sales;
proc sql noprint;
select avg(Salary)
   into :MeanSalary
   from orion.employee_payroll as p,
        orion.employee_organization as o
   where p.Employee_ID=O.Employee_ID
         and Department=Propcase("&Dept");
reset print number;
title  "&Dept Department Employees Earning";
title2 "More than the Department Average "
       "of &MeanSalary";
select p.Employee_ID, Salary
   from orion.employee_payroll as p,
        orion.employee_organization as o
   where p.Employee_ID=O.Employee_ID
         and Department=Propcase("&Dept")
         and Salary>&MeanSalary;
quit;
title;
```

74

Using Macro Variables to Make Your Program Dynamic

1. Retrieve the program **s108d06**.

2. Change the value assigned to the macro variable **Dept** in the %LET statement to **Engineering** and
   submit the program.

```
%let Dept=Engineering;
proc sql noprint;
select avg(Salary)
   into :MeanSalary
   from orion.employee_payroll as p,
        orion.employee_organization as o
   where p.Employee_ID=O.Employee_ID
         and Department=propcase("&Dept");
reset print number;
title  "&Dept Department Employees Earning";
title2 "More than the Department Average "
       "of &MeanSalary";
select p.Employee_ID, Salary
   from orion.employee_payroll as p,
        orion.employee_organization as o
   where p.Employee_ID=O.Employee_ID
         and Department=Propcase("&Dept")
         and Salary > &MeanSalary;
quit;
title;
```

3. Examine the results in the Output window.

PROC SQL OUTPUT

	Engineering Department Employees Earning		
	More Than The Department Average Of 30698.33		
	Row	Employee_ID	Salary
	1	120117	31670
	2	121016	48075

The average and the results from the query are populated dynamically by making one simple change from **Sales** to **Engineering** for the value of **Dept**. To generate another report with different values, simply make one change to the value of **Dept** and the program is capable of making the substitutions dynamically at the appropriate places within the code.

Creating Multiple Macro Variables: Syntax 1

Using the INTO clause, create multiple macro variables that contain the minimum, average, and maximum salary for the entire company.

```
select avg(Salary),min(Salary),max(Salary)
   into :MeanSalary, :MinSalary, :MaxSalary
   from orion.Employee_payroll;
%put Mean: &MeanSalary Min: &MinSalary
     Max: &MaxSalary;
```

Partial SAS Log

```
Mean: 38041.51 Min:    22710     Max:    433800
```

77   s108d07

 Exercises

If you restarted your SAS session since the last exercise, open and submit the **libname.sas** program found in the data folder.

Level 1

4. Creating and Using Macro Variables

a. Write a query for the **employee_payroll** table that returns the highest value of **Salary** (**max(Salary)**). Title the report as indicated in the sample output.

PROC SQL Output

```
                    Highest Salary in employee_payroll


                              _____
                               433800
```

b. Use %LET statements to create and assign values to two macro variables:
DataSet = employee_payroll
VariableName = Salary

Use a %PUT statement to write their values back to the SAS log in this context:

SAS Log

```
NOTE:  DataSet=Employee_payroll, VariableName=Salary
```

c. Modify the query you wrote in **4.a**. Replace each hardcoded (typed) reference to **employee_payroll** (once in the title and once in the query) with a reference to the macro variable **DataSet (&DataSet)**. Replace each hardcoded (typed) reference to **Salary** (once in the title and once in the query) with a reference to the macro variable **VariableName (&VariableName)**. Resubmit the query, and verify that the results are identical to the results obtained in **a.** above.

d. Use the %LET statements to change the values of your macro variables:

DataSet = Price_List
VariableName = Unit_Sales_Price

Run the report again. The results appear below:

PROC SQL Output

```
                 Highest Unit_Sales_Price in Price_List


                              _____
                               630.4
```

Level 2

5. Creating a Macro Variable from an SQL Query

a. Produce a report of **Country** and a new column named **Purchases (SUM (Total_Retail_Price))**. Group the report by **Country**. Include only orders placed in 2011. Order the report so that the highest values of **Purchases** sums are at the top. The data is in the following tables (columns of interest in parenthesis):

- **Order_fact (Customer_ID, Total_Retail_Price)**
- **Customer (Customer_ID, Country)**

Name the report **2011 Purchases by Country**. Label the columns as indicated in the sample report:

PROC SQL Output

```
                        2011 Purchases by Country

                               Customer
                        Country     Purchases
                        _____
```

US	$10,655.97
CA	$5,210.5
AU	$3,902.49
ZA	$1,954.1
TR	$961.4
DE	$429.6
IL	$194.6

b. Write a query similar to the first but modified to produce a report of **Purchases** by **Customer_Name** for the year 2011. (Keep a copy of your first query for use in **5.c.**below.) Subset the query so that only customers from the top-buying country (the one listed at the top of the last report; in this case, **US**) are included. Order the report so that customers with the highest purchases are at the top. The data is in the following tables:

- **Order_fact (Customer_ID, Total_Retail_Price)**
- **Customer (Customer_ID, Customer_Name, Country)**

Name the report **2011 US Customer Purchases** with a second title line of **Total US Purchases: $10,655.97** as indicated by the previous query. When you run the report, it should produce the following results:

Partial PROC SQL Output

2011 US Customer Purchases	
Total US Purchases: $10,655.97	
Customer Name	**Purchases**
Karen Ballinger	$3,479.09
Cynthia Martinez	$1,777.60
Cynthia Mccluney	$1,093.60
Wynella Lewis	$736.60
Alvan Goheen	$728.80

c. Automate the report that you wrote in **5.b.**

1) Modify the query from **5.a.** so that instead of producing output, it merely writes the values for **Country** and **Purchases** for the first returned row into macro variables named **Country** and **Country_Purchases**, respectively.

2) Modify the query that you wrote in **5.b.** by substituting the macro variable reference **&Country** for each instance where you typed the value **US** in the query, and the macro reference **&Country_Purchases** in the second title line in place of the **$10,655.97** value that you typed previously. When you are finished, run the modified queries. The results should be exactly as produced in **5.b.**

Hint: Do not forget to use double quotation marks around macro variable references. Review syntax 1 for inserting values into macro variables, if necessary.

d. Starting with the code from **5.c.**, modify the first query so that the country with the lowest total purchases is read into the macro variable instead of the highest. Then rerun both queries. The queries should produce the following results without further modification:

PROC SQL Output

2007 IL Customer Purchases	
Total IL Purchases: $194.60	

Customer Name	Purchases
Avinoam Zweig	$194.60

Challenge

6. Using Dictionary Tables and Macro Variables to Build Low-Maintenance Code

Create a program that, when provided with a libref and the name of a table column, locates in the specified library all of the tables that contain the named column, and writes a custom SQL query that joins them all, producing an output table.

Use the program **s108e06** as a starting point. This is a partially completed utility program that will, when completed, identify all of the tables in any user-specified library. Then join them based on a user-specified common key column to produce a single output table. Your job is to complete the first three steps of the program, which create and populate the macro variables required by the fourth (already completed) section of the program. The fourth section of the program demonstrates SAS macro programming techniques that are outside the scope of an SQL class. Do not modify this section until you successfully completed the exercise.

In **6.a.** below, you write a query to create a macro variable and store the number of tables in the specified library that contains the common key column. In **6.b.**, you write a second query that creates a series of macro variables storing the names of the individual tables. In **6.c.**, you write a third query that creates a single macro variable containing a comma-delimited list of all the tables that contain the common key column.

The two %LET statements near the top of the program assign values to two macro variables: **Library** and **JoinVar**. When you write your portion of the program, reference those values (**&Library**, **&JoinVar**) wherever you type the SAS library libref or the column name in your program code.

Following the %LET statements, there are three sections reserved to write each of the three queries necessary to complete the program. They are clearly labeled with comments: **Query 1:**, **Query 2:**, and **Query 3:**. Remember not to edit the already completed macro program code that follows these sections.

a. In the section reserved for Query 1, write a PROC SQL query that counts the number of tables in **Library** that contains the column **JoinVar**. Write that value to a macro variable named **Rows**.

b. In the section reserved for Query 2, write a PROC SQL query that creates a series of macro variables named **Table1**, **Table2**,... **Table***N* (that is, one for each of the tables in **Library** that contains the column **JoinVar**). You should use the macro variable **Rows**, created in the previous query, to determine the number of macro variables that you need (*N*).

c. In the section reserved for Query 3, write a PROC SQL query that creates a macro variable named **SourceTables**. **SourceTables** must contain a list of the fully qualified names of all of the tables in **Library** that contain the column **JoinVar**. The names should be separated by commas. The contents should resemble the following: **LIBRARY.Table1, LIBRARY.Tables,... LIBRARY.Table***N*.

d. After you create your queries, run the entire program. Review the SAS log. There should be only one error message located near the bottom of the SAS log.

Partial SAS Log

```
ERROR:  ************* JoinTheTables Macro *********************
ERROR:  Column Some_Column_Name not found in any of the ORION tables
ERROR:  ************* JoinTheTables Macro *********************
```

e. Near the top of the code, change the value assigned to **JoinVar** in the %LET statement to **Customer_ID** and rerun the program. Review the SAS log and explore the table produced by the program to answer the following questions:

   1) What is the name of the table produced? _____

   2) How many columns does the table contain? _____

   3) How many tables contain the column **Customer_ID**? _____

f. Change the value assigned to **JoinVar** in the %LET statement to **Product_ID** and rerun the program. Review the SAS log and explore the table produced by the program to answer the following questions:

   1) What is the name of the table produced? _____

   2) How many columns does the table contain? _____

   3) How many tables contain the column **Product_ID**? _____

8.4 Solutions

Solutions to Exercises

1. **Using PROC SQL Options and Displaying the Contents of a Dictionary Table**

   a.

```
*** s108s01 ***;
proc sql flow=6 35;
title "Dictionary Tables";
select distinct memname,memlabel
   from dictionary.dictionaries;
quit;
title;
```

   b.

```
proc sql;
title "Tables containing Customer_ID";
select Memname, Type, Length
   from dictionary.columns
   where libname="ORION"
         and upcase(Name)="CUSTOMER_ID";
quit;
title;
```

2. **Using PROC SQL Options and Displaying Dictionary Table Information**

a.

```
*** s108s02 ***;
proc sql flow=6 35;
title "Dictionary Tables";
select Memname as Table, Memlabel as Contents,
        count(*) as Columns
   from dictionary.dictionaries
   group by Table, Contents;
quit;
title;
```

b.

```
proc sql flow=6 35;
title "Orion Library Tables";
select memname "Table",
        nobs "Rows",
        nvar "Columns",
        filesize "File Size",
        maxvar 'Widest Column',
        maxlabel 'Widest Label'
   from dictionary.tables
   where libname='ORION'
         and memtype ne 'VIEW'
   order by memname;
quit;
title;
```

3. **Using PROC SQL Options, SAS System Options, and Dictionary Tables to Document Data Tables in the Orion Star Library**

```
*** s108s03 ***;
  /**************************************************
    This query remerges summary data and will not work
    if OPTIONS SQLREMERGE=NO is in effect.
    **************************************************/

options ls=85 ps=20;

proc  sql flow=2 25;
title "ORION Library Table Information";
footnote "* Largest in the Library";
select memname "Table",
        cats(nobs,
            case
                when nobs=max(nobs) then "*"
                else ""
             end) "Rows",
        cats(nvar,
            case
                when nvar=max(nvar) then "*"
                else ""
```

```
                    end)  "Columns",
         cats(put(filesize,comma12.),
               case
                   when filesize=max(filesize) then "*"
                   else ""
               end) "File Size (Bytes)",
         cats(maxvar,
               case
                   when maxvar=max(maxvar) then "*"
                   else ""
               end) 'Widest Column'
     from dictionary.tables
     where libname='ORION'
           and memtype ne 'VIEW';
quit;
title;
footnote;
```

4. **Creating and Using Macro Variables**

   a.

```
*** s108s04 ***;

proc sql;
title "Highest Salary in Employee_payroll";
select max(Salary)
    from orion.employee_payroll;
quit;
title;
```

   b.

```
%let DataSet=employee_payroll;
%let VariableName=Salary;
%put NOTE:  DataSet=&DataSet, VariableName=&VariableName;
```

   c.

```
proc sql;
title "Highest &VariableName in &DataSet";
select max(&VariableName)
    from orion.&DataSet;
quit;
title;
```

   d.

```
%let DataSet=Price_List;
%let VariableName=Unit_Sales_Price;
proc sql;
title "Highest &VariableName in &DataSet";
select max(&VariableName)
    from orion.&DataSet;
quit;
```

```
title;
```

5. Creating a Macro Variable from an SQL Query

a.

```
*** s108s05 ***;
proc sql;
title "2011 Purchases by Country";
select Country,
       sum(Total_Retail_Price) format=dollar10.2 as Purchases
   from orion.customer as c,
        orion.order_fact as o
   where c.Customer_ID=o.Customer_ID
     and year(Order_Date)=2011
     group by Country
     order by Purchases desc;
quit;
title;
```

b.

```
proc sql;
title  "2011 US Customer Purchases";
title2 "Total US Purchases: $10,655.97";
select Customer_Name,
       sum(Total_Retail_Price) format=dollar10.2 as Purchases
   from orion.customer as c,
        orion.order_fact as o
   where c.Customer_ID=o.Customer_ID
         and year(Order_Date)=2011
         and Country="US"
     group by Customer_Name
     order by Purchases desc;
quit;
title;
```

c.

```
proc sql noprint;
select Country,
       sum(Total_Retail_Price) format=dollar10.2
       into :Country, :Country_Purchases
   from orion.customer as c,
        orion.order_fact as o
   where c.Customer_ID=o.Customer_ID
         and year(Order_Date)=2011
     group by Country
     order by Purchases desc;
reset print;

title  "2011 &Country Customer Purchases";
title2 "Total &Country Purchases: &Country_Purchases";
select Customer_Name,
       sum(Total_Retail_Price) format=dollar10.2 as Purchases
```

```
      from orion.customer as c,
           orion.order_fact as o
    where c.Customer_ID=o.Customer_ID
          and year(Order_Date)=2011
          and Country="&Country"
    group by Customer_Name
    order by Purchases desc;
quit;
title;
```

d.

```
proc sql noprint;
select Country,
       sum(Total_Retail_Price) format=dollar10.2
       into :Country, :Country_Purchases
    from orion.customer as c,
         orion.order_fact as o
    where c.Customer_ID=o.Customer_ID
          and year(Order_Date)=2011
    group by Country
    order by Purchases /* ascending requires no keyword */;
reset print;
title  "2011 &Country Customer Purchases";
title2 "Total &Country Purchases: &Country_Purchases" ;
select Customer_Name,
       sum(Total_Retail_Price) As Purchases
       format=dollar10.2
    from orion.Customer as c,
         orion.Order_fact as o
    where c.Customer_ID=o.Customer_ID
       and year(Order_Date)=2011
       and Country="&Country"
    group by Customer_Name
    order by Purchases desc;
quit;
title;
```

6. Using Dictionary Tables and Macro Variables to Build Low-Maintenance Code

a.

```
*** s108s06 ***;
  /* Warning: Case sensitive! */
%let JoinVar=Some_Column_Name;
%let Library=%upcase(ORION);
proc sql noprint;
select strip(put(count(*),5.))
       into :Rows
    from dictionary.columns
    where libname="&Library"
          and name="&JoinVar";
quit;
```

b.

```
proc sql noprint;
select memname
        into :Table1-:Table&Rows
    from dictionary.columns
    where libname="&Library"
          and name="&JoinVar";
quit;
```

c.

```
proc sql noprint;
select catx('.',libname,memname)
        into :SourceTables separated by ','
    from dictionary.columns
    where libname="&Library"
          and NAME="&JoinVar";
quit;

    /************************************************
        For the exercise, do not edit below this line!
     ************************************************/

    /************************************************
     This macro program joins all the tables in Library
     which contain the column JoinVar by JoinVar, producing
     a table called Joined_By_JoinVar. By default, the table
     is created in the work library. For example, if
        JoinVar = Employee_ID
     then the table produced is
        work.Joined_by_employee_id
     ************************************************/

options mprint;
%Macro JoinTheTables(OutLib);
%if &OutLib= %then %let OutLib=work;
%if &Rows gt 1 %then %do;
    %do i=1 %to &rows;
        proc sql noprint;
            select catx('.',"&&Table&i",Name)
                into :&&Table&i.._Columns separated by ","
                from Dictionary.Columns
                where libname="&Library"
                      and MEMNAME="&&Table&i"
                      and Name ne "&JoinVar"
            ;
        quit;
        %end;
    %put _user_;
    proc sql;
    create table &OutLib..Joined_by_&JoinVar AS
        select &&Table1..&JoinVar
```

```
    %do i=1 %to &Rows;
        %let ThisColumn=&&&Table&i.._Columns;
        , &&&ThisColumn
    %end;
        from &SourceTables
        where &Table1..&JoinVar=&Table2..&JoinVar
    %do i=2 %to %eval(&Rows-1);
        %let j=%eval(&i+1);
        and &&Table&i...&JoinVar=&&Table&j...&JoinVar
    %end;
    ;
    quit;
      %put NOTE:  ************ JoinTheTables Macro ************;
      %put NOTE:  Column &JoinVar found was found in &Rows tables;
      %put NOTE:  ************ JoinTheTables Macro ************;
    %end;
    %else %if &Rows=1 %then %do;
      %put NOTE:  ************ JoinTheTables Macro ************;
      %put NOTE:  Column &JoinVar found only in               ;
      %put NOTE:  &Library..&Table1 table                     ;
      %put NOTE:  No join could be performed                  ;
      %put NOTE:  ************ JoinTheTables Macro ************;
    %end;
      %else %do;
        %put ERROR: ************ JoinTheTables Macro ************;
        %put ERROR:  Column &JoinVar not found in any          ;
        %put ERROR:  of the &Library tables                    ;
        %put ERROR:  ********** JoinTheTables Macro ************;
      %end;
%mend;

%JoinTheTables;
```

d. No solution is required.

e. For the **Customer_ID** column:

  1) What is the name of the table produced? **work.Joined_by_Customer_ID**

  2) How many columns does the table contain? **22**

  3) How many tables contained the column **Customer_ID**? **4**

f. For the **Product_ID** column:

  1) What is the name of the table produced? **work.Joined_by_Product_ID**

  2) How many columns does the table contain? **24**

  3) How many tables contained the column **Product_ID**? **5**

Solutions to Student Activities (Polls/Quizzes)

Discussion

What is wrong with the following code?

```
proc print data=dictionary.tables label;
   var memname nobs nvar;
run;
```

**In SAS procedures or the DATA step,
the libref cannot exceed 8 characters.**

15

8.01 Quiz – Correct Answer

In your SAS session's SAS Explorer window, navigate
to the **Sashelp** library by selecting **Libraries** ⇨ **Sashelp**.
Scroll down to examine the **Sashelp** views.

Which view shows the names and data types of all the
columns in every table available in the SAS session?

SASHELP.vcolumn

18

8.02 Multiple Answer Poll – Correct Answer

Specifying the NOEXEC option in a PROC SQL statement does which of the following?

(a.) prevents statement execution for the current invocation of PROC SQL

   b. applies only to the SELECT statement

(c.) checks SQL query syntax without actually executing the statements

   d. displays rewritten PROC SQL statements after references are expanded and certain other transformations are made

31

8.03 Quiz – Correct Answer

Without re-invoking PROC SQL, add a statement before the second query that does the following:

- displays output rows without row numbers
- ensures that only nine rows are output

```
reset nonumber outobs=9;
```

This statement displays output rows without row numbers and ensures that only nine rows are output without re-invoking PROC SQL.

40

8.04 Quiz – Correct Answer

How many changes must be made to the program to generate a report showing how many Engineering Department employees earn above-average salaries?

One. Modify the value assigned to the macro variable Dept in the %LET statement.

```
%let Dept=Engineering;
```

75

Chapter 9   Learning More

9.1 SAS Resources

Objectives

- Identify the areas of support that SAS offers.

3

Customer Support

SAS provides a variety of resources to help customers.

http://support.sas.com/resourcekit/

4

Education

SAS Education provides comprehensive training, including

- more than 200 course offerings
- world-class instructors
- multiple delivery methods
- worldwide training centers.

http://support.sas.com/training/

5

SAS Global Certification Program

SAS Education also provides

- globally recognized certifications
- preparation materials
- practice exams.

http://support.sas.com/certify/

6

Networking

Social media channels and user group organizations enable you to

- interact with other SAS users and SAS staff
- learn new programming tips and tricks
- get exclusive discounts.

For training-specific information:

http://support.sas.com/training/socialmedia

7

SAS Books

SAS Books offers a complete selection of publications, including

- eBooks
- CD-ROM
- hard-copy books
- books written by outside authors.

http://support.sas.com/bookstore/

1-800-727-3228

8

Extended Learning Pages

To grow your SAS skills, remember to activate the *extended learning page* for this course.

Individual learning software licenses are available through SAS® OnDemand for Professionals: Enterprise Guide.

http://support.sas.com/learn/ondemand/professionals

9

9.2 Beyond This Course

Objectives

- Identify training opportunities to build on the skills you learned in this course.

11

Next Steps

SAS® SQL 1: Essentials provides portable skills that are useful in most of the focus areas shown below.

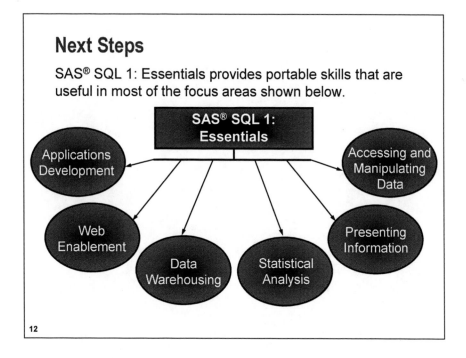

12

Next Steps

To learn more about this:	Enroll in this course:
Writing self-modifying, environmentally aware, easily maintained SAS programs	SAS® Macro Language 1: Essentials
Efficiently working with real world data	SAS® SQL2: Processing Data Efficiently in Real-World Scenarios
Efficiently preparing data for data mining and analysis	SAS® Programming 3: Advanced Techniques and Efficiencies
Creating tabular detail and summary reports	SAS® Report Writing 1: Essentials

13